8-85

D0729576

# Julio

ELIZABETH GARCIA

BALLANTINE BOOKS · NEW YORK

Library of Congress Catalog Card Number: 85-90558

ISBN: 0-345-32349-1

Cover photo: Frankie Ziths/Star File Photos
Cover design by James R. Harris
Interior of book designed by Michaelis/Carpelis

Manufactured in the United States of America

First Edition: August 1985
10 9 8 7 6 5 4 3 2 1

A mis padres sin cuyo apoyo y su cariño
esta labor hubiera sido imposible.

# CONTENTS

# ACKNOWLEDGEMENTS

A very special thanks to Donna McCrohan for her invaluable support and guidance, without which this book never could have been completed.

Many thanks to José Manuel Cuevas and Emilio N. García; to interviewees Ramón Arcusa, Manuel De La Calva, Alfredo Capalgo, Enrique Garea, Rafael Díaz Gutiérrez, Gerhard Haltermann, Tony Renis, and Rafael Revert; to photographers Manolo, Juan Rivera, and Juan Ruiz. I would also like to thank Anne, Vanna, Ze, Jo, Marguerite, Luzia, Mandy, Donna, Nydia, Maria Julia, Grace, Sathie, Anna, Nadya, Maria, Raúl, Carmen, Hilda, Fabian, Gerry, Denise, Fred, Edson, Rafael, Kyoko, Elba Rosa, Pota, Paul, José, and Betty.

# INTRODUCTION

*A* year or two ago, just about any U.S. journalist might easily have written of Julio Iglesias, "Who is he?"

But in the summer of 1984, Wayne Robins, in New York's *Newsday*, wrote, "When Michael Jackson grows up, maybe he'll be as popular as Julio Iglesias."

It would seem that Julio Iglesias experienced a startling leap into superstardom. But nothing could be further from the truth. True, prior to 1984 his name was definitely NOT a household word throughout the U.S.A. Still, throughout the other nations of North, Central, and South America and much of the rest of the world, the name "Julio Iglesias" was ringing in every home— the result of years of hard work.

Before his record-breaking U.S. successes even began in the summer of 1984, Julio was the bestselling artist in the worldwide history of the recording business. He had ranked number one in more than sixty countries. His records had outsold those of Barbra Streisand and Michael Jackson. His face had been featured in upwards of 15,000 magazines.

He'd appeared on over 800 television programs in sixty-nine countries; given over 2000 live concerts; privately performed for heads of state ranging from President Reagan and Princess Grace to the Aga Khan; and won hundreds of gold and platinum records, in six languages. He was the only artist ever awarded the Diamond Disc by the *Guinness Book of World Records* for record sales topping one hundred million, the all-time worldwide high.

Then, two of the sharpest predictors of American tastes—Johnny Carson and the Coca-Cola Company—had given him the nod. Johnny had brought Julio on his show and raved about him. And Coca-Cola had signed him to a multimillion-dollar contract, sponsoring his seven-month, six-continent concert series in exchange for Julio's participation in some Coke commercials.

Already the claim could be made that every thirty seconds, someone somewhere in the world was listening to a Julio Iglesias song. Now, the stage was set for his "meteoric overnight success" in Denver, Los Angeles, New York, and the rest of America.

If this success was overnight, it would have had to have been the longest night of the year.

His name has indeed now become a household word in the U.S.A. The proof? Joan Rivers observed, speaking at a recent luncheon for Nancy Reagan, "My idea of foreign affairs is a motel with Julio Iglesias."

# THE
# PHOENIX
# YEARS

Julio Iglesias was born on September 23, 1943. (September 23 is also the birthday of Bruce Springsteen, Ray Charles, and Mickey Rooney.) In 1943, despite the war, or perhaps as a brief escape from it, the world was watching the unforgettable Humphrey Bogart and Ingrid Bergman movie *Casablanca*, which immortalized a ballad later to enter Julio's repertoire: "As Time Goes By."

Julio's mother was Rosario ("Charo") de la Cueva. His father was eminent Spanish gynecologist Dr. Julio Iglesias-Puga. Julio Jr. was their firstborn child. His birth, in Madrid, Spain, was the stuff of legends, for, according to one popular rumor, he cried out from his mother's womb. It's a theme associated with the world's most legendary conquerors.

But unlike the world's legendary conquerors—and despite the fact that his maternal grandfather, Jorge José de la Cueva, was the author of Spain's beloved army song—Julio Iglesias was not a man of battle. Growing up as he did in the immediate wake of

Spain's bitter Civil War, he bore only the emotional scars of his nation's recent tragedy. In this, he and his generation of Spaniards have more in common with our country's "baby boomers," born in the late 1940s and early '50s, than with Americans born, as he was, during World War II.

In the years shortly before Julio was born, Spain had a king, but a king in exile. Spain was a "worker's republic"—a very unstable one. In 1936, a number of factions rose up to contest the government and each other. They fought on Spanish soil. Even the capital city—Madrid, the city of Julio Iglesias' parents—was laid siege. Throughout the country and in the capital, lands were ravaged and families destroyed. Food was scarce. Sickness was rampant. The economy was in chaos.

In the course of Spain's agony, a soldier by the name of Francisco Franco appeared on the scene. He rose through the ranks to take control, restoring "peace" by means of a reign of terror. Accounts released by Madrid prisons indicate some 500 executions took place every week during 1939 and 1940.

The Civil War, which had begun in 1936, was officially over in 1939. But the terror continued. Spain's penal population was in the hundreds of thousands. In Madrid, there were fourteen formal prisons, and schools were converted into detention facilities. In the same city, five permanent courts-martial were convened, charging defendants with acts of participation in leftist political parties. Those found guilty of treason were sentenced to death by firing squad.

No sooner was the Civil War over than Spain was being courted by the Allies and the Axis Powers to join the Second World War. Though Spain was officially neutral, she effectively sided with the Axis, sending the "Blue Division" to fight side by side with Hitler's Germans in the 1941 invasion of Russia. When the Axis lost, Spain was in worse trouble than before.

In the early 1940s, Spain was a country recovering from war in a world torn apart by war. The living conditions, especially for the lower classes, were miserable.

By the mid 40s, things were improving, relatively speaking. Generalísimo Franco—who, in order to win the Civil War, had led half of Spain to attack the other half—was still dictator of Spain, with mass executions tapering off to "only" a few thousand per year. Though even these numbers still seem inconceivable, it was an improvement to most Spaniards. Death no longer loomed so large over every doorstep. Besides even a bloody dictatorship was welcome after the years of civil war.

People who had lived through the nightmare were hardened to just about anything but a repeat of it. Their relief, their willingness to live under oppression, had nothing to do with politics. Most Spaniards will tell you that politics have absolutely nothing to do with patriotism, that, regardless of any political situation, it's the destiny of a Spaniard to want to live in, and be in love with, Spain.

It was this world, this ideological legacy, into which Julio Iglesias was born. He was shaped by the tragic and joyous experiences of his motherland. This explains why today, as a man, he is so passionately drawn to the U.S. ideals of liberty and freedom, yet at the same time in love with the country of his birth.

Though his parents had lived through the Civil War, Julio never saw its horror. Like any child who has nothing to compare things with, he took it for granted that his world was precisely the way the world should be.

"Like all kids," recalls Julio, "I was mischievous. I did what I was told, and I tried to study as little as possible, though trying to get good grades at the same time."

This sounds as normal as a childhood could be. Julio did have what might be considered the advantages of a normal childhood by American standards, yet it was well above the norm for a Spanish child of his generation. He went to school at Los Sagrados Corazones (The School of the Sacred Hearts), at a time when as many as 50 percent of Madrid's children never went to school. He had a healthy childhood, while in the postwar years, nearly three quarters of Madrid's children were tubercular. His mother recalls that he didn't have a gigantic appetite (though he was decidedly partial to her fried potatoes and tortillas españolas), at a time when a full stomach was a luxury in parts of Spain.

As he grew up, he enjoyed the benefits of progress that the government channeled into Madrid, the country's capital. Buildings and parks went up on a grander scale than anywhere else in Spain. Plays that were prohibited elsewhere in Spain—for instance, the sexually charged work of Tennessee Williams—were available to the residents of Madrid. Tourists poured into Julio's city, bringing with them their foreign tastes and cultural awareness.

Perhaps the greatest tragedy of Julio's youth was merely (and ironically!) that he was rejected by the choir of Los Sagrados Corazones. (They should see him now!) Such were the normal tragedies in the life of an ordinary young boy.

His greatest triumphs as a youngster were on the soccer field. His interest in soccer began as a hobby but developed into more. He showed real promise, and soon was spending hours at the sport to sharpen his skills. By the time he was fourteen, he was a dedicated athlete; his drive and energy were infinite. As yet, he had no interest in music other than as a passive listener.

By the time he was seventeen, Julio was attending law school, in training to be a diplomat, at the behest of his father. (His younger brother, Carlos, was set to be a doctor.) But Julio was more interested in soccer, having now become something of a popular hero playing semiprofessionally as goal keeper for the Real Madrid (Royal Madrid) team.

Then, suddenly, real tragedy struck. When he was twenty-one, while Julio was driving his sports car through the outskirts of Madrid, a freak accident all but claimed his life. His car went out of control and skidded off the road, pinning him underneath, and seemingly smashing his spine. His back was destroyed. He was close to death. He was rushed to the hospital for fourteen hours of delicate surgery that spared his life but left him paralyzed.

Initially, two thirds of his body were immobile. He couldn't use his hands. To get around, he was dependent on a wheelchair. Julio's father consulted with top specialists in the field, who were divided in their prognoses. Some felt that Julio would recover eventually. Others were totally pessimistic about his future.

Julio, confined either to his bed or his wheelchair, had little desire to live. His days of playing soccer were finished. It seemed he might never even walk again.

During his convalescence, Eladio Magdaleno, a male nurse, gave Julio a guitar to distract him from his depression, and as therapeutic exercise for his fingers. With this, Julio slowly began to improve, shaking his fears and becoming more and more confident that full recovery was within his grasp. As his spirits picked up, so did his musical flair. Soon he was singing and composing his own songs. Miraculously, within twenty months, he was on his feet—not completely recovered, but able to get around on his own. Julio and Eladio Magdaleno, who worked with Julio's father, remain friends to this day.

Of the nightmare, Julio has since said, "God placed me in that situation of total suffering, to later give me what I have today. . . . After seeing death so close, I was reborn."

Like the mythical phoenix, the bird that died in fire and was reborn from its own ashes, Julio Iglesias was reborn from his near-fatal accident. Moreover, he was reborn with a gift he might otherwise never have known he possessed, the gift of song.

Walking again, and with a song in his heart, Julio Iglesias tried to put his life together. Luckily, he still had his legal studies. He could still become a diplomat. His father sent him to prestigious Cambridge University in England to continue his education in law.

To this day, Julio regrets not having mastered the English language at that time, but he was distracted by another student. An attractive, French, female student. Before long, she was playing an important role in his emotional life, and inspiring him to write beautiful love ballads. During this time, his French improved dramatically—something that enabled him, in later years, to break into the French music market and record in *their* language.

Also during this time, just for fun, he was playing guitar and singing for friends in the college pubs of Cambridge. Sometimes they'd tell him to try to sell his songs to record companies or big recording artists. Never before had he seriously considered making money from music. But all in all, it didn't seem like such a bad idea.

In 1968, while attending a party for the Eurovision Song Festival in London, Julio Iglesias introduced himself to Manuel de la Calva and Ramón Arcusa. These two singer/composers enjoyed a fine artistic reputation in Spain, where they were known as El Dúo Dinámico (the Dynamic Duo). They recall their first meeting with Julio fondly.

Manuel de la Calva tells us, "We were in London because our song 'La, La, La' had been selected to represent Spain in the festival. There had been some controversy over the song because originally it was to have been sung by Joan Manuel Serrat. However, Serrat insisted on singing the song in Catalán. Spanish television felt that the song should not be sung in Catalán since that isn't the official language of the country. Serrat withdrew and Massiel took his place.

"Julio bumped into us in the hallway of the hotel where the party was being held. He hadn't even begun to record as of yet. Anyway, he came over to us and said, 'Aren't you Manuel and Ramón? Listen, I want to tell you something. I was at the rehearsals and your song is going to win.'

"Just like that. Then Julio went on to say, 'And another thing. Before the year is out, you are going to hear about me because I am going to sing.'"

Ramón Arcusa adds, "What he said came true. We won the festival, and within a year he was known in Spain."

When Julio returned to Spain from England, he presented himself at Discos Columbia, not once but repeatedly. Still recovering from his accident, he was on crutches. Gerhard Haltermann, then Promotion Director at Discos Columbia, recalls, "He spent about six or seven months going to see our Artistic Director, Linda B. Meredith. Iglesias would sing the songs that he had composed and tried to convince her how good they were. She finally agreed to sign him on. Even back then he was very ambitious. But that is a great part of his success."

Julio recorded his long "La Vida Sigue Igual" (Life Continues All The Same). Enrique Garea, A&R Manager (later General Director) of Discos Columbia, explains, "Augusto Alguero, the musical director, and I came up with the title of that song. The song itself was written by Julio. The arrangement was by Pepe Nieto. Manolo Galvan, who now lives in Argentina, was the leader of the group Los Gritos (The Shouts), the group that would soon perform the song with Julio. They were already a successful, well-liked group."

The song was a good one, and the decision was made to have him compete at the Tenth Spanish Song Festival in Benidorm. The Benidorm Festival is enormously visible and significant in the musical life of Spain, something like a "Star Search" on a grand scale. A Benidorm winner commands great respect.

To Julio, who had just graduated law school, this meant a door opening, and a decision to be made. He struck a deal with his father, who wanted him to enter the legal field without delay. It was agreed that Julio would enter the Benidorm contest. If he won, he could try his luck at a career in professional singing. If he lost, he'd forget about singing and be a lawyer.

He entered the festival, on July 16, 17, and 18, 1968, nervous and wearing trousers that were a little too short. Barely out of the recording studio after having made his demo record, he was anything but a polished pro. He had considerable difficulty with the orchestra during rehearsals. On the first day of the competition, he was the first one to perform, accompanied by Los Gritos. There are those who remember that Enrique Garea had to gently coax him onto the stage, warning, "Get out there or I'll kick you out there," and that Julio stumbled out with his hands plunged deep into his pockets.

But despite his lack of experience and his case of nerves, he came out a finalist. By the third night of the Benidorm Festival, he was the victor, winning not only for his song, but also picking up an award for Best Interpreter.

Manuel de la Calva and Ramón Arcusa were in the audience, witnessing that the second of Julio's predictions had come true.

From Benidorm, Julio went on to participate in songwriting contests around the world, in countries like Italy, Romania, Guatemala, and Japan. His musical career was soon an established fact. And, although he was a fully qualified, licensed attorney, his legal career never got off the ground.

His life differed completely from anything that he or his parents had anticipated, though it's fair to say of his sixteen-year international music career, that he became a multilingual Diplomat of Song.

# THE
# NEW
# DON JUAN

*A* foreigner, not knowing better, will look at the Spanish flag and say, "Oh, yes, its colors are red and yellow." But not the Spaniard. Red? Yellow? Not in the least. The Spaniard looks at the flag and sees crimson and gold.

Crimson, the color of passion, calls up images of the blood that beat in the heart and coursed through the veins of the legendary Don Juan. The gold, the brilliant gold, is the sun that smiled on Don Quijote's impossible dream.

In his heart, every Spaniard is a son of Don Juan. In his mind, he is Don Quijote, daring to believe in the wildest of dreams. Julio Iglesias was a Spaniard in the truest sense of the word.

For the aspiring Don Juan of the 1960s in Spain, there could have been no more promising avenue than an international career in music. It provided exposure to women all over Europe, perhaps all over the globe. Better still, it provided the opportunity to talk love to every woman in every audience, to run up a mile-long list of women swooning for a man they'd never formally met. It also offered a Spaniard the chance to get away, from time to time, from the restrictions of Spanish customs, without ever having to declare any sort of separation from Spain.

Indeed, for any Don Juan, Spanish customs of the heart were highly restrictive, particularly compared to what was going on in the rest of Europe. It did not always look this way, however, to the casual observer, as traditionally, the Spanish man was expected to bestow *piropos* on beautiful women who passed by. *Piropos* are compliments of an extremely specific, even graphic, sexual detail, called out to strangers. A man who wasn't free with his *piropos* was often considered less than a man. But everyone knows that *piropos* are just talk.

The *piropos* were only one facet of public morality. Public propriety, which frowned on things like kissing on the street, was another. A third was censorship. In Spain, with one of the world's highest ratios of cinemas to population, even the poorest people flocked to the movies, not only for the escapism afforded, but also for the soft seats, air conditioning in the summer, and heat in the winter. And what did the people *see* when they got to the movies? Censored love scenes!

So rare was public display of passion that a big kiss on a movie screen could be expected to provoke loud stomping, whistling, and shouting from adult men. Anything sexier than a kiss—for instance, a tempestuous embrace in an imported film—would in all probability be snipped out by the censors. A pair of screen lovers might be seen approaching each other with open arms yet, a second later, be loading groceries into a truck. What happend in between was left to the Spanish imagination!

When not scissoring, the censors would be dubbing foreign films. Remember the 1953 movie *Mogambo*, starring Clark Gable and Grace Kelly? It told the story of a hunter, his wife (Kelly), and the safari leader (Gable). Predictably, the wife and the safari leader fall into deep, forbidden love. But what did the censors turn this triangle into? They turned it into a story about a hunter, his *sister*, and a safari leader. The love between Kelly and Gable was forbidden because "my brother is a close friend of my fiancé, who is ill in a hospital in London."

Though Spain's censorship was phased out after Franco died

in 1975, its presence was acutely felt by everyone of Julio's generation. It had been an intrinsic part of Spanish life for more than a generation.

Contrast this ambiance with the international scene of the jet set, and it's easy to see why a Spanish Don Juan would enjoy conducting some of his romances abroad.

Today, reviewers are quick to proclaim Julio Iglesias the new Don Juan, or, as Stephen Holder calls him in *The New York Times*, "the traditional Latin Lover incarnate."

Sometimes, reviewers go a step further, heralding him as the "Valentino of the '80s." To a Latin, this is one of the highest compliments, for Rudolph Valentino was the first Latin to become a sex symbol on the American silver screen. They conveniently forget that Valentino was ridiculed by people who didn't appreciate him, and consumed by the harsh pressures of his fame. Valentino died at the age of thirty-one. But try for a moment to visualize an aged Valentino. It's impossible. To some extent, Rudolph Valentino preserved his image as a sex symbol by dying young. For that matter, Don Juan didn't live to an old age either. The legendary romantics didn't want to grow old.

Today Julio Iglesias is past his fortieth birthday. One of the things he says to his audience when performing in the U.S. is "Why did you wait so long to discover me?" or variations on that theme. When people call him a sex symbol, he says that he's "just a skinny guy in a T-shirt." But to fans, he's not getting older, he's getting better, in the style of Cary Grant. Like Grant, he projects an image of elegant sophistication and ingratiating charm. These manly qualities draw fans like a magnet. But Julio can also look like he's pushed himself too hard. Then his fans want to protect him, to mother him, to keep him out of trouble— a mixed blessing for a sex symbol or a Don Juan.

Early in his career, Julio Iglesias had all the incentive in the universe to emulate Don Juan. His name was linked amorously with an impressive roster of lovely ladies, one of whom became his wife.

But as his career blossomed, another dream formed in his mind that increasingly dominated his interests and activities. It was a dream more than worthy of the same Don Quijote who inspired Julio's song "Quijote" on the *Momentos* album, which went on to be number one in more than ninety countries. Julio's dream was to conquer the U.S. music market—the most influential market of them all, and the toughest, particularly for someone who doesn't speak the English language like a native. Speaking of his dream, Julio told reporters, "To a performer there's something about making it in America that's just impossible to describe. It's always been my dream." Arma Andon, vice president of product development for Columbia Records, noted of Julio that "He is completely devoted to breaking America. He eats, sleeps—and sings—breaking America."

Today Julio has achieved his dream, and having done so, he offers dreams to others. "My goal is to make people dream. When they see me onstage, their fantasy of me and the reality meet. I seduce them. But I must seduce myself first."

# ONE
# LONG
# SONG

*W*hen Julio first opened his mouth to sing "La Vida Sigue Igual" at Benidorm, in 1968, he began a serenade to the world that has never ended. For some, it would have been enough to achieve what Julio had by 1971, or 1975, or 1980, or 1983. But for Julio, with his eyes squarely fixed on the U.S. market, there would be no easing up.

His formal recognition first came on the night of July 18, 1968, when he won the Song Festival at Benidorm. That was the birth of Julio Iglesias the artist, the man who would conquer the music world over the next sixteen years.

Upon Julio's return to Madrid, Discos Columbia began to work closely with their new artist. Like all promising new artists joining a record company, Julio got "the works." Photos were made for distribution to the national press, along with an up-to-date bio.

Julio's first single, "La Vida Sigue Igual," was released in September 1968. With it, Julio immediately captured the hearts of his fellow countrymen (and countrywomen!) and was soon competing on the charts with such gifted top-selling artists as Raphael,

Joan Manuel Serrat, Tom Jones, Englebert Humperdinck, the Moody Blues, and the Rolling Stones.

Julio had the good fortune to have signed with a record company that believed in him, though certainly his own enthusiasm and drive rubbed off on those around him. He was to record thirteen albums in the eleven years that he was associated with Discos Columbia. The first release, *Todos Los Días Un Día*, set off fireworks.

Once the album was completed, a tour was scheduled in Spain. Between radio programs that had to be taped or done live, and interviews for magazines and newspapers, Julio hardly had a minute to himself. His newfound career was exhausting work, but it seemed to be the work he was born to do. Said Julio at the time, "I like people. . . . Perhaps other artists don't enjoy being surrounded by people, but I do."

It was early in his career that Julio, having done so well at Benidorm, was sent to another festival. This one was the famed Viña del Mar, in Chile. For Julio, it was far more than an important introduction to the South American public. It was an introduction to the V.I.P.'s of the Latin music industry, who would be attending the festival. In both Latin and European music markets, many a singer has been "discovered" or propelled into a major career by the international coverage accorded Viña del Mar. It is also undeniable that the audiences at the Viña del Mar festivals are very demanding. A singer who makes a hit at Viña stands a good chance of sweeping the surrounding countries.

One Chilean journalist who saw Julio perform that year at Viña del Mar predicted that he was going to be the top Latin singer in the world. Julio laughed. But today, Chile is one of the countries in which Julio's records sell best.

In fact, Julio holds a special fondness for the Chileans, which they return. Viña's local drink, *pisco,* made with the local *aguardiente* ("fire water"—made from fermented grapes, sugar, and lemon), the *empanadas* (oven-baked as compared to the empanadas of most Latin countries, which are fried), the *locos* (not crazy people, but abalone), *corvina* (whitefish), *erizos del mar* (sea urchins)—all rank high on Julio's list of favorites. Add to this Viña's sun and sea, and it's easy to understand why Julio visits whenever possible.

When he returned to Madrid, Julio began work on his first motion picture, titled, not surprisingly, *La Vida Sigue Igual*. No masterful autobiographical work, it was at least a pleasant romp through the early years of Julio's life. It explored his days as a goal keeper for the Real Madrid, the car accident and recovery, his discovery of the guitar, his first attempts at singing and composing, and, finally, the Benidorm competition. This film, along with a second one, *Todos Los Días Un Día* (All The Days In A Day), occasionally turns up on Spanish television. However, film acting wasn't Julio's chosen career, and he rarely speaks of these movies today.

Closer to Julio's heart at the time—as Enrique Garea, General Manager of Discos Columbia, recalls—were charity benefits. Julio often offered his services to help out needy organizations. On one such occasion, Julio filled a school hall with an audience of 2000, in order to raise money for clothing for the poor. Both Julio and the group Los Bravos (known for their international hit "Black Is Black") performed there for free.

In time, the list of benefit performances increased. The Red Cross invited Julio to perform in Guatemala. Soon, he would be appearing around the world, for a wide range of worthy causes.

No performing artist can function properly in today's highly competitive musical arena without sufficient business support. Julio is no exception.

At the beginning of his career, Julio's manager was Enrique Roca. Roca, an Argentinian, was part of a group called Quique Roca and Claudia. The group was highly successful on a national level, but when Roca joined Julio's camp, he stopped performing in order to manage Julio exclusively. Julio's association with Roca was eventful but short-lived. It wasn't long before the two went their separate ways.

After Enrique Roca, Julio worked with his second manager, Enrique Herreros. By all accounts, Herreros handled Julio well and worked hard, making significant contributions to Julio's career. Some feel he was more prominent in his field than was Julio at the time. Today, Herreros is involved in films, while Alfredo Fraile, who worked with Herreros, went on to become Julio's third manager.

In 1970, Enrique Herreros, Enrique Garea, and Gerhard Haltermann (Promotions Director at Discos Columbia) convinced Bernard Chevry, director of MIDEM (Marché International De Disque Et De L'Édition Musicale—International Record and Music Publishing Market), to invite Julio to be a guest singer for the gala that would kick off the week-long events. MIDEM is "staged" for the music industry, specifically, for record manufacturers and publishers. It gives them the opportunity to discuss and negotiate future projects. It could also be described as a week of wheeling, dealing, and gastronomical delight. Since 1966 it has been held on the last week in January in Cannes, France, and is yet another component of the lifeblood of European music. The 1970 MIDEM was a great leap forward for Julio, giving him greater exposure, greater success, and greater acclaim.

Along with Julio's recordings, his movie, and his MIDEM, media, and charity appearances, he continued to participate in song festivals.

Song festivals like Benidorm and Viña del Mar are an integral part of the Latin and European music world, not to be overlooked by any singer desiring visibility and respect. Festivals can be unpredictable yet, commercially, an effective springboard for recognition. Julio Iglesias went to San Remo, and while he did not make the top spot, he gained valuable exposure.

In February 1970, Julio participated in another festival, this time in Barcelona, Spain. It was at this event that artists were chosen to represent Spain at the Eurovision Festival in Amsterdam, the Netherlands. To qualify as an entry, a song had to be new and original, and it had to be sung by two artists. All told, there were twenty titles. The two people to sing Julio's song were Julio and the Armenian singer Rosy Armen, who had come to Spain the year before.

A friend recalls that Julio's father was present at this festival, cheering his son along and telling everyone that the young man on stage was going to be the next Frank Sinatra. People thought he was an overzealous father, and dismissed the prediction with a laugh. They even claimed the comparison was absurd after Julio won and went on to the Eurovision festival. Today, Dr. Iglesias has the last laugh. His son is often referred to in the U.S. as "the Spanish Sinatra." Rob Baker in the New York *Daily News* wrote, "Iglesias has the most extraordinary pop male singing voice since Sinatra, and with more heat and feeling than Old Blue Eyes ever had."

But back in 1970, in those days in Barcelona and the Netherlands, a widely accepted comparison with Sinatra was years away. This was particularly so in terms of stage presence. Friends remember that Julio was still in the habit of walking on stage with his hands in his pockets. It's rumored that his tailor, at the request of Discos Columbia, made a suit without pockets for Julio's Eurovision appearance. At the time, it seemed to break him of the habit.

At Eurovision, Julio sang "Gwendolyne," the song that had won in Barcelona. It had been written to the great love of his Cambridge days. He did not win the top place, though he took fourth position in the finals. It almost seemed not to matter. He'd gained a valuable introduction to the neighboring European countries participating in the festival, another stepping-stone en route to worldwide recognition.

It was at this point in Julio's career that Discos Columbia decided to record his singles in different languages. By doing this they hoped to accelerate his crossover to other countries. "Gwendolyne" was recorded in London not only in Spanish but also in English, French, and Italian, and became a hit throughout Latin America and Europe. Since then, "Gwendolyne" has been re-recorded by artists like Marco Antonio Muñiz of Mexico and Chucho Avellanet of Puerto Rico, adding yet another laurel to Julio's crown.

As Julio's popularity increased, so did his professional commitments. Though he didn't enjoy flying and still doesn't, the pattern quickly established itself that flying and being Julio Iglesias are inseparable. Once, early in his career, he was offered an appearance on Italian television, for no pay. The exposure was thought to be compensation enough. Despite his dislike of flying he took off immediately, acutely aware of the doors it might open to his future in different territories. Today, Julio practically lives on a plane. And they come to him almost as often as he to them!

Once Julio received an invitation from a very important European television network. He promised to appear, then found himself without transportation when an airline strike effectively closed the skies. The television station did not hesitate to send him their private plane. That's how much in demand he had become.

If 1970 did not find Julio to be the world's busiest man, it at least found him in the top 500. He was, it seemed, entirely too busy to fall in love. But he was a Spaniard at heart, part Don Quijote, part Don Juan. When he met the right woman, busy or not, he fell.

# EARLY YEARS

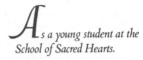

*A*s a young student at the
School of Sacred Hearts.

Agencia Efe

C*ould he be girl watching?*
*(right) Out for a stroll. Dr. Iglesias,*
*wife Rosario, sons Carlos and Julio*
*(below). Oh, that million-plus smile*
*(bottom right).*

Imapress/Pictorial Parade, Inc.

Manolo

Manolo

Manolo

C an't keep his eyes off the ladies (above). With composer Manuel Alejandro who co-wrote, with A. Magdalena, two Julio hits, "Así Nacemos" and "Manuela" (right).

Manolo

Manolo

*A*t one of his early recording sessions (left). Dr. Iglesias and Julio standing outside the house where famed bullfighter Manolete was born (below).

# DON JUAN
# TIES THE
# KNOT

By 1970, Julio was a full-fledged star, and with stardom came his entry into the international jet set. It suited him. He enjoyed good times and great parties.

At one such party, at a friend's house, in May 1970, Julio caught his first glance of the woman who would later be his wife. Julio found it difficult to tear his eyes from her exquisite beauty, with her Oriental aura and distinctive style. He was desperate for an introduction but couldn't arrange it that night.

He made inquiries, and discovered she was from the Philippines and that her family was in the business of representing American companies such as Coca-Cola and 3M. Her family was friendly with the Philippine ambassador to Spain. She was in Madrid to study and to be introduced to the Spanish aristocracy. Her beau at the moment was the Marquis of Griñón.

Her name was Isabel Preysler.

During this time, Julio was recording in London on weekends and dating an actress who had worked with him in the film *La*

*Vida Sigue Igual.* His career had definitely taken off, and he was working constantly.

A friend invited him to another party. Because of his recording commitment, Julio declined, but when he learned that Isabel was going to be at the party, he changed his tune. Once he got to the party, he made it his business to be introduced to her. Despite the fact that he had won a series of international song festivals, despite his record sales and his brief movie career, Ms. Preysler didn't seem terribly impressed with Julio Iglesias the singer.

It took Julio a while to get her phone number, and even then not directly from Isabel. But the man was persistent, and once he had the number, he called Isabel and invited her out. She agreed, and they went to a Juan Pardo concert. It proved to be a lovely evening, which quickly led to an affectionate relationship. Soon they were seeing each other as often as possible, having to schedule themselves around Julio's work demands.

A friend of Julio's—a co-worker from his first record company—recalls the way Julio's face lit up whenever he described the wonderful Isabel. Though he did his best to contain himself, Julio was clearly enthralled. Isabel was different than the other girls he'd known. She was exotic. She was THE ONE.

He fell for her—much harder at first than she fell for him.

Julio wanted to spend each and every moment with Isabel. But now his career was going full throttle, taking him on frequent tour, often out of the country. His meetings with Isabel were fewer, while his phone bills climbed and climbed.

As the phone bills skyrocketed, their love grew, and with it, their desire to be together.

Absence must have made the heart grow fonder, because Julio gathered up the courage to propose. Isabel said no. But the second time he asked, she was his.

They married on January 20, 1971, in a chapel in the Spanish province of Toledo. They honeymooned in the Canary Islands. Within a year, they had begun their family.

Isabel helped Julio immensely at the beginning of his career. She was very disciplined, a complete perfectionist. Something of this rubbed off on Julio, remaining with him in his life and work even today.

Isabel traveled with Julio on his tours. According to a reliable source, it was the efforts of Julio and Isabel Iglesias, not the efforts of the record company, that opened the door to Julio in Latin America. It was the Iglesiases' relentless pursuit of the Latin American market that established Julio there. This was especially true in Mexico, to which Julio and Isabel, along with Julio's manager, Alfredo Fraile, went four or five times at a financial loss, staying at affordable hotels, all financed out of Julio's own pocket. He performed in as many places as humanly possible, on some evenings giving two performances. His day wouldn't end until early morning. Isabel was an integral part of the fabric of his life, morally, psychologically, and mentally.

He paid her the highest tribute: "Respect is almost as important as love. You have to admire your companion." Julio admired her, listened to her advice, and acknowleged her help in reinforcing his image to the public.

Their hard work paid off. By 1971, Julio Iglesias had sold one million records.

Julio and Isabel continued in their close, loving relationship. He was often heard to say that she was a splendid woman, that "she respects everything, she moves me, and I am more in love with her than when I married." Once he was quoted as saying, "Fidelity to me is like a vaccine. I don't believe I'll ever find anyone better than my wife. She fills my life. . . . I married forever."

# THE

# CONQUEST

# CONTINUES

Soon Julio was appearing before crowned heads. In 1970, he had performed for Princess Grace of Monaco and the Aga Khan at Puerto Banus in Spain. He also ventured beyond his previously established bounds, competing in (but not winning) for instance, the famed Osaka festival in Japan.

The Mexican and other Latin American markets, difficult to enter at first, were no longer a problem. Julio had gained the enthusiasm and respect of these very diverse audiences.

In 1971, he made a second tour to Japan, accompanied by Enrique Garea. There he recorded his first song in Japanese, "Antamo Uramo" (originally the Spanish "Como El Alamo Al Camino"—Like A Poplar to the Road). It wasn't a great success, especially not compared with his later tremendous impact in Japan, but it *was* an inroad.

Nineteen seventy-one was also the year that his first child, Chaveli, was born. Though born prematurely, Chaveli was a beautiful, healthy girl. Julio was a proud, excited daddy, and to this day, he shows a special affection for her in his songs. Chaveli appears with him on the cover of the album *De Niña A Mujer* (From a Child to a Woman). The album has since appeared on the U.S. charts. Its title song was inspired by and is dedicated to Chaveli.

In 1972, Julio recorded his first song in Galician, a lyrical language spoken by natives of Galicia, Spain. Called "Canto a Galicia" (Song to Galicia), it represented an effort to again expand his market by singing in yet another language. Some locals, of Galician origin and descent, reproached Julio for not pronouncing all the words correctly. It was said that the song was, at best, half Galician and half Spanish. Despite such criticism, it became a success, reaching huge sales in countries like Germany, the Netherlands, and Belgium. It reached charts in Latin America, North Africa, and the Middle East. In time, it became so successful that the criticism had to subside. The most ardent diehards acknowleged that Julio Iglesias was singing the praises of Galicia throughout Europe. He includes the song in his repertoire, singing it with great affection, even today.

In the same year, Julio's first album in German was released. Gerhard Haltermann recalls accompanying the artist to Germany to tape a television program. Says Haltermann, "The audience honestly believed that he understood and felt every word he was singing. Of course, his pronunciation when done live wasn't always perfect, yet at the exact moment, he would give just the right intonation. They loved it when he sang the word 'heart' in German. Everyone would go wild because they genuinely felt he knew exactly what he was saying."

In that year, 1972, in recognition of his wide-ranging successes, Discos Columbia bestowed upon Julio Iglesias their award for "Top Record Seller at Discos Columbia."

The following year, 1973, Isabel Preysler de Iglesias gave birth to a brother for Chaveli. Feeling that a man is more helpful in the delivery room than outside in the waiting room (a thought perhaps gleaned from his gynecologist father), Julio was present at the moment of the arrival of his second child, Julio José, into the world.

With two young children in tow, and Julio's career expanding every day in a new direction, Isabel was finding it more difficult to travel with her famous husband. Whenever possible, she joined him. But it was most often not possible.

Julio's record sales were now up to ten million (only 990 million to go before earning the *Guinness Book of World Records* Diamond Disc!). He seemed unbeatable. But success took its toll. The demands imposed on him by his career were greater and greater. He was on the road all the time, while Isabel and the children stayed home. It was very trying, yet he remained very human.

Enrique Garea remembers a touching anecdote from about this time. It happened during one of Julio's many tours to Mexico. Julio was doing a television show in Mexico City with Argentinian singer Alberto Cortez. The two decided to do a duet, with Julio singing Alberto's songs and Alberto singing Julio's. It was, for the audience, a memorable evening. To one in the audience, it was a dream come true. There was a young girl sitting out among the others, in a wheelchair. Perhaps as a gift of optimism, in memory of his own days of confinement, Julio stopped the program to give her his gold chain. This moment, witnessed on national television, went right to the heart of the nation. It was touching, it was human, it was very real. It was not, however, unique for Julio, who has revealed this side of himself on any number of occasions throughout his career.

During these years, Julio was enjoying ever-increasing popularity in South as well as Central America. Alfredo Capalgo, one of Argentina's foremost empresarios, promoters, and producers, scheduled Julio whenever possible. Julio was *big* there, but nowhere near as big as he wanted to be.

Recalls Alfredo Capalgo, "There's a street in Buenos Aires, very important, very famous. It's called Florida. The street is primarily made up of movie houses. It's always crowded with people. One day Julio asked me to take him there, to see if anyone would recognize him. We went to that street, and no one gave him a second glance. Julio thought about it and told me that he'd only be important the day he could walk down Florida Street and everyone would know him. On his third trip to Buenos Aires, he asked me to take him back to Florida Street. It was amazing.

It was impossible for him to get near it. He had become their idol."

It stood to reason that once Julio Iglesias was this popular in the Spanish-speaking world, his success would filter into Spanish-speaking communities of the United States. When Julio's fans from abroad visited family and friends in the U.S., they'd bring his records as gifts. When Latin Americans and Europeans living in the U.S. would visit foreign soil, they'd stock up on Julio's latest hits abroad. So it developed that, long before Julio reached U.S. shores, he had a U.S. following. With U.S. census figures reflecting an Hispanic-American population of about 20,000,000, it was possible for Julio to captivate millions of U.S. fans without specifically aiming a recording at the U.S. market. It was a suitable springboard for what would ensue.

The year 1974 brought Julio to the U.S., face-to-face with the world's biggest record market. And just when it seemed that there was no stopping him—that he'd called every shot to perfection, not making a single, solitary wrong move—a misunderstood remark, never intended to offend, exploded into an obstacle of monstrous proportion.

The result was to put the U.S. market, for a time, right out of Julio's reach.

# CLOSE CALLS
# IN NEW YORK
# AND MIAMI

*I*n 1974, one of the most respected promoters in the New York area was Rafael Díaz Gutiérrez. Currently, he is part owner of the very successful and popular Latin radio station WSKQ in New York and Los Angeles radio station KSKQ.

He clearly remembers the events surrounding Julio's first Miami appearance, and the events that took place prior to, during, and after his debut in New York.

"Julio had an unfortunate incident take place during his first appearance at the Montmartre nightclub in Miami. A remark that he made had been misinterpreted by a few Cubans who were present. Julio, in an attempt to ingratiate himself with the audience, told them that as he was singing to them that evening, he would like to sing to their fellow countrymen in Cuba. A spectator in the front row—the man had had more than his share of drinks—threw his glass at the artist. A commotion ensued and the club's administrator, Mr. Cabrisas, was unable to placate the crowd.

"Julio was then escorted out of the club for fear of his safety.

Afterwards, it was wrongly concluded by some, on the basis of that one remark, that Julio was a Communist. Of course, he never said he wanted to sing to Castro. It was obvious that he meant he wanted to sing to the Cuban people. However, because of this incident, it was considered something of a risk to bring Julio Iglesias to the United States."

People who worked closely with Julio at Discos Columbia point to Betty Pino as one of the most important figures in his life in the days surrounding the unpleasant incident in Miami. She fought hard to secure air time for him when there was a ban on his records at the radio stations. These were dark days for Julio, and her support was invaluable.

Discos Columbia, Julio's record company, was concerned about what was happening. It was vital to overcome the Miami setback, which affected not only the Miami audiences but also potential audiences throughout the nation.

The company was very anxious to break Julio into the New York area, as well as to correct the impression left by the Miami mishap. Columbia sent over Tomás Toral (major shareholder and husband of company president Aurora Inurrieta), Enrique Inurrieta (Managing Director, and brother-in-law of Toral), and General Manager Enrique Garea to feel out the situation. They proceeded to interview a series of promoters in the hopes of negotiating a mutually satisfactory agreement. They approached Carnegie Hall and Lincoln Center in order to obtain a reputable and prestigious site for Julio's debut in the New York area. However, as Rafael Díaz Gutiérrez explains, "They soon discovered that the only dates Julio had free to perform weren't available at either theater. There was one date, but I was already down for it. After a number of meetings, I agreed to relinquish the date over to them.

"The date that was being considered was the same date that Julio was scheduled to appear in Miami. It was a very important engagement, since he was trying to win back the public in that area. The only solution was to have him perform in New York in the afternoon, and in Miami the same evening.

"I was happy to work with him, and I think he was happy and

grateful that I had taken the challenge of representing him. I'm Cuban. So working with him was a statement in itself. I didn't believe for a minute that the accusations against him were true. They had no validity, no foundation. Beyond believing that he was no Communist, I believed in him as an artist. His talents are unique.

"When his concerts were announced, we were flooded with threats. There was one date in New Jersey that we had no choice but to cancel, because we were unable to pacify the Cuban residents in the area.

"Nonetheless, the New York concert date was set, and it sold out. Discos Columbia paid for all the expenses—the rental of Carnegie Hall, the musicians, and extra security, including dogs trained in sniffing out bombs. Every imaginable precaution was taken for safety's sake.

"We picked Julio up at the airport. We were immediately captivated by him. He seemed very down to earth, a little nervous, and excited about his upcoming debut on one of the most important stages in the world. Julio was unaware of the bomb and death threat against his life. On the way to rehearsal, he made an interesting remark. He said, 'This is a great city and I've longed so much to perform here. And I will conquer this city when she discovers that I am humble and sincere.'

"Because his schedule was so tight, no press conference was held. At rehearsals, Julio was cooperative and much more relaxed than he'd been at the airport. In my thirteen years as a promoter, only two artists opened with a dark stage and only a spotlight on themselves. One was Argentina's Sandro. The other was Julio Iglesias."

Julio sang accompanied by twenty-eight of New York's finest musicians; Maestro Rafael Ferro conducted. At his charismatic best, Julio mesmerized an international audience. Besides singing in Spanish, he sang in Galician, French, Italian, and even ventured into English. In the course of the concert, he made two clothing changes. By the show's end, he had the audience on its feet, yelling bravo and urging him to do encore after encore. He gave them as much as he could, but could not go on forever, since he had to catch a plane to Miami.

The show closed on a note of complete triumph. Despite the threats, no one had been hurt. Yet as Julio, Rafael Díaz Gutiérrez, and other members of the contingent left the theater, they were advised that a large crowd had gathered outside. The news was greeted with mixed emotions, but the crowd turned out to be far from hostile. The crowd was made up of members of the audience who had just witnessed the debut, and of well-wishers and admirers who had been unable to obtain tickets.

Says Gutiérrez, "Once we saw them, there was no question that Julio could have had another sold-out concert in New York. We were escorted by the police from Fifty-seventh Street to Fifty-fifth Street. Everyone was in a wonderful mood. It was quite beautiful and a very touching farewell to the artist. We were pleased to have been able to participate in his triumph. The following day, the ban on his records was lifted and he was being heard in both Miami and New York."

Gutiérrez remembers Julio saying to him, while en route to the airport, "I don't know if I conquered the city of New York, but I think I entered the hearts of all who saw me."

Rafael Díaz Gutiérrez still holds a high regard for Julio Iglesias. "He's alone in what he's done. He's been able to project himself on an international market. Few Latin performers have been able to come close to such recognition. It will be difficult for another artist to top him."

From New York, Julio continued directly on to Miami, but, the serious threats against him continued too. Julio was nervous, and confided to Enrique Garea that he didn't know how he was going to be able to sing. But he did . . . and beautifully. The show went on as scheduled, without a hitch. It was a triumphant comeback, leaving no doubt that Julio Iglesias was loved in Miami.

# FAMILY/PRIVATE
# REWARDS

Richard Young/Retna Ltd.

*A*t the Málaga Football Stadium Julio sang a special song to his daughter Chaveli (left). Julio was honored in Paris with a wax likeness at the Grévin Museum (above). Serenading former wife Isabel Preysler during happier times (right).

AGIP Pictorial Parade, Inc.

Manolo

Agencia Efe

*S*tanding proudly with
Queen Sofia and King Juan
Carlos of Spain (right).
Julio, Chaveli, Julio José,
Enrique, and Isabel at Bara-
jas Airport in Madrid
(below).

Manolo

Manolo

Imapress/Pictorial Parade, Inc.

*J*ulio, Alfredo Fraile
(Julio's former manager),
journalist Jesús Marinas,
Chaveli, Enrique, and Julio
José are introduced to the
King and Queen of Spain
(above). Dr. Julio Iglesias,
Julio's father (left).

Peter C. Borsari

Manolo

The Bettmann Archive

*W*ith Chaveli at the Albert Ein-
stein Award Dinner honoring Kirk
Douglas (upper left). Taking on
Paris with Isabel (above). Julio and
Hey at their estate in Indian Creek
in Florida (left).

The Bettmann Archive

*D*r. Julio Iglesias during a press conference in Miami describing his kidnapping by the Basque Separatist group ETA (left). Julio celebrated his 40th Birthday at the Pre Catalan in Paris where he was honored by friends. Happy Birthday Julito (below)!

AGIP/Pictorial Parade, Inc.

# SEVEN

# TRIUMPH AT MADISON SQUARE GARDEN

Julio and Isabel's son Enrique was born in 1975. Again, Julio stood by Isabel's side in the delivery room. And again, soon after, he was traveling.

Julio was steadily seeking and conquering new territories. In Mexico, where he'd once gone to such enormous effort to establish himself, he was now so popular that he found himself compelled to take sixteen suits on his tours. This was because fans were suddenly storming the stage, pulling at and tearing his clothes. Sometimes the suits could be repaired. Sometimes they were beyond help. His wardrobe, in piecemeal fashion, was being converted into instant souvenirs.

Julio's tours were taking him to North Africa, the Orient, and North America. The competition was enormous. Julio couldn't relax his guard for a moment. He's said to be a workaholic, a perfectionist, a fighter, and a disciplined and demanding artist. But without that drive, that striving to surpass himself as an artist, he wouldn't be the bestselling artist he is.

Only in the summer time would Julio be able to spend time

with his family. Gerhard Haltermann, who worked closely with Julio as the Promotion Director at Discos Columbia, remembers these happy times. "I often spent my summers in Torremolinos, and Julio and his family had a chalet about ten kilometers away. Every summer, we'd meet and Julio would always invite me and my family to join them. I'd be in the water with his kids and mine, and we'd have great fun. I don't believe the children have ever wanted for anything. Chaveli is a very open child. She was very charming even back then. She had an English nurse who looked after her. The boys were great fun too. They were very small at the time, and I haven't seen them in a while. Once they got to know you, they were very warm. The Iglesias family appeared to be a very united family."

Julio has often shared such moments, precious moments spent with his family, with the press. The charge has been leveled that he uses his family to enhance his public image. But anyone seeing him with his family would find it hard to agree.

Julio has said that the love of a father for his child should be the least selfish and impartial of all. Sadly, he was also quoted as saying that he couldn't help feeling his career was chipping away at his marriage and his family life.

Of Isabel, he often commented that she was 90 percent of their marriage. As the years went by and Julio's fame spread, perhaps neither Isabel's 90 nor Julio's 10 percent were enough to sustain their happiness.

Says Enrique Garea who worked closely with Julio for eleven years, "I believe Isabel collaborated with him whenever possible. Keep in mind that he was traveling incessantly. He wasn't home much. He never lived an intense family life. Once his career took off, he'd see his children every three months. His career always came first. He was very ambitious and wanted to succeed."

Julio has often remarked that he questioned how his success and career could possibly compensate for his personal losses. He always counted on Isabel's strength and steadiness, and took it for granted that her exceptional qualities would balance any strain. Unfortunately, there was too much strain, too many demands pulling Julio in too many different directions. His absences became longer and longer. His fans were seeing much more of him than did his children and his wife.

Julio's career was moving very fast. . . .

Julio's successes, his triumphs, fell into place one after another. His recording of "Manuela"—written by Spanish composer Manuel Alejandro, who was responsible for Spanish singer Raphael's string of hits, and A. Magdalena—caught on in Europe, North Africa, and Latin America. In France alone it sold over 500,000 copies.

In 1976, Julio was responsible for making *El Amor* the biggest-selling album ever in Argentina and Colombia—*and* for breaking a box office record at Madison Square Garden. For this show of shows, his popularity among the Spanish-speaking public drew crowds not only from the New York area but also from New Jersey, Connecticut, Massachusetts, Philadelphia, and Washington, D.C. It was completely sold out, despite the fact that Julio still had no U.S. releases under his belt.

With Julio's Madison Square Garden coup, the press was heaping new accolades on him. "The new Valentino" became one of their favorite phrases for describing his appeal. Says Alfredo Capalgo, "It's an interesting comparison. One of Julio's secrets is his eyes. They're not the eyes of a Spaniard. His look reminds me of Rudolph Valentino. A Spaniard's expression around the eyes can be timid, subdued. But Julio has a very aggressive expression with his eyes. Like Valentino, he can communicate volumes with them."

Manuel de la Calva re-entered Julio's life when he became Artistic Director of Discos Columbia. In this capacity, he was involved in choosing the repertoire that the artist would record. Additionally, he produced and co-wrote, together with his partner Ramón Arcusa, and of course with Julio. As before, the "Dúo Dinámico" (De la Calva and Arcusa) had to marvel at the talents of the young man who had approached them in a hallway in London nearly a decade ago, foretelling his professional future with uncanny accuracy.

In January 1977, Enrique Garea went to Germany with Julio

because Discos Columbia had begun to release all his records there. In Germany, Julio appeared with the Berlin Philharmonic. The building was like a temple. Inside, Julio stood in the middle of the orchestra, singing primarily in Spanish. When he sensed that his Spanish songs were not bringing the German audience close to him, Julio switched languages. To everyone's surprise, he launched into the song "Bahia"—in Portuguese. It wasn't what anyone had expected. But Julio was a hit.

Later, in 1977, Julio's popularity was so great in Chile that he filled the Estadio Nacional (National Stadium) in Santiago with 80,000 fans, breaking all attendance records for that country.

By the time 1978 rolled around, Julio was a super-selling recording artist, a performer who could draw SRO crowds, and a jet-setter who regularly traversed several continents. But then, he'd been working at it for a full decade. It was anyone's guess what the next decade would bring.

# EIGHT

# THE
# KNOT
# UNTIED

*A*s Julio moved from triumph to triumph, he told an interviewer, "My success demands more of me, there are more countries to go to, more things to leave behind. I have to look at things more rapidly, the embraces are shorter."

The decade beginning in 1978 promised to be the Julio Decade. Julio Iglesias, not Goldfinger, was the man with the Midas touch. It seemed that every record he touched turned to gold, with some even going platinum.

But one aspect of his life wasn't golden. His marriage was coming apart.

Julio was in his early thirties, strikingly handsome, and an international star. His fans had good reason to want to see him, not only on stage, but at the stage door and anywhere else an admirer might fantasize being with her heartthrob número uno. Like any other performer of the stature Julio had attained, he was at the center of a spectacle not on any concert program—the spectacle of women throwing themselves at him.

And after all, Julio Iglesias was and is a Spanish heir to the legacy of Don Juan, an alter ego particularly appealing for a Spaniard abroad.

An aide who traveled with Julio describes these days with a laugh of great pleasure. "I don't know what he's like now, but back then he'd drive us crazy. He wanted his Peruvian girlfriend to meet him in Germany, then the German one was to be in Japan, and the Japanese girlfriend was to join him on his tour in South Africa. I don't know how *he* did it, but for us, it was tiring. Finally I couldn't stand it and I suggested that he 'go domestic' wherever we went. The expenses involved were steep and, needless to say, came right out of Julio's pocket."

But the biggest problem wasn't what came out of Julio's pocket. The biggest problem was what came out to the public, and how. Depending on the tone and the timing, any behavior by a public figure can look innocent in the press, or damning.

For Isabel Preysler de Iglesias, her seven-and-a-half-year marriage to Julio Iglesias was no longer working out. She may have been Julio's Rock of Gibraltar, but her heart wasn't made of stone.

She asked for a divorce. In Spain, a country quite close to the Catholic church and very conservative, divorces were discouraged. Moreover, in Spain, a country with *macho* roots going back a thousand years, a woman was expected to accept any vagaries of marriage as her lot. In the centuries when the Moors held sway in Spain, and the religion was Mohammed's, morality included the possibility of four legitimate wives for a man and as many concubines as he could support. In the twentieth century, with the Moors long gone from Spanish soil, their influence lingers on.

The woman who speaks up is liable to be put down. This is what happened to Isabel Preysler de Iglesias. She was the wife. Julio was the husband. And he was the star, known by the press and well liked. In the main, the media (90 percent male, in Spain) sided with Julio as the wronged party. In truth, both parties were the victims of something that, ironically, they'd both worked together for—Julio's multicontinental career.

In the beginning, it bound them as few couples ever could be united. In the end, it was the very thing that made it impossible for them to be together.

Julio has said his career wasn't the wedge that separated him from Isabel, but rather that people change with time.

It's true that times change, and time changes people. As his and Isabel's lives evolved differently so had their preferences and interests. Certain things accelerate the effect of time on people—for instance, a lifetime of experience packed into every year, and exposure to more people in a month than most people meet in a lifetime. There can be no doubt that Julio isn't the man he'd have been had he hung out his shingle and practiced law. Certain sacrifices were unavoidable. His personal life was rarely his own. People were endlessly vying for his time and attention. What little time he had with his family was dear to him, and painful to surrender.

"Failure" is a word rarely found in Julio's vocabulary, though he's been known to use it when referring to his marriage. "A strong human tax" comes up too—the tax paid to underwrite his mind-boggling worldwide success.

Says a close friend of Julio's, "Their split is the one thing I don't think he's ever accepted. I've known him to take plenty in his stride. Never that."

What Julio did do was sing about lost love and heartbreak, in a way that, ironically, took the public by storm. When he sang to "that woman" or "that mother-in-law," fans responded with compassionate affection. When he sang "Hey"—about being in love with someone who doesn't love you back—the fans were in the palm of his hand.

Asked recently to identify the woman of "Hey," in an interview conducted by his ex-wife Isabel Preysler, Julio explained that the song is a sort of general confession, with nobody personalized in it. In 1984, it might well be a generalization. But back then, the public perceived it very personally. This perception served to enhance its popular appeal.

In a way, it was like Eddie Fisher recording "Arivederci, Roma," when his wife, Elizabeth Taylor, left him for Richard Burton during the making of the movie *Cleopatra* in Rome.

"Hey" produced an immediate wave of sympathy that sustained itself for close to two years.

The dissolution of the marriage became official in 1978, with Julio steadfastly maintaining his respect for Isabel and that "I haven't forgotten she is the mother of my children."

With this major change in Julio's life came other significant transitions. Not only did he throw himself into his work, but he also acquired a residence in Miami, Florida. By now, he had negotiated and finalized a contract with CBS Records, by which the company would represent him worldwide.

He sent for his children, who joined him in Miami for a very special holiday of joy as well as sadness. They went to Disney World in Orlando, but they also talked about what had happened to Julio and Isabel. That is, Julio spoke about it to his daughter, his oldest child, Chaveli. The boys were still too young to understand, and had less of an adjustment to make, since they'd never known what it was like to have their father around for an extended period of time.

When their visit was over, Julio again threw himself into his work. He wrote, he recorded, he sang. He studied to perfect his Italian, Portuguese, German, and Japanese, with an eye on each of those markets.

The Don Quijote in Julio "Don Juan" Iglesias was going strong. Whatever markets adored him, whatever continents were tapping their toes to his songs, there was still work to do. There was still the United States of America. There was still the impossible dream.

# GOLD, IN ANY LANGUAGE, IS GOLD

*I*n 1978, Julio decided to make a career move, signing with CBS International. An established and respected artist around the world, he was a worthy addition to the CBS roster. From CBS, Julio could look forward to absolute worldwide promotion, a logical step for someone with his eyes so unwaveringly fixed on the U.S. market.

A second career move brought him in contact with Ramón Arcusa, who became his producer. Together they penned, along with Manuel de la Calva, "Soy Un Truhán, Soy Un Señor" (I'm A Rogue, I'm A Gentleman). Recorded in several languages, it became an international hit.

Working with Ramón Arcusa, Julio did *Aimer La Vie* (To Be in Love with Life), his first French album. It sold 740,000 copies. His album *A Mis 33 Años* (To My 33 Years) went gold when it hit the 50,000 mark in the Netherlands. Simultaneously, it became a hit throughout Latin America. His first Italian album, *Sono Un Pirata, Sono Un Signore* (I'm A Pirate, I'm A Gentleman) instantly climbed the charts in Italy.

In 1979, Julio recorded his first album in Portuguese. Throughout that year, he continued to tour the countries that contributed so much to his success—the nations of Latin America, Europe, the Middle East, Canada, and the U.S. cities where his following was strong. His various distinctions were now considered more than sufficient to earn him an invitation to Australia to judge the Miss Universe contest.

When he returned to Miami, Julio recorded the album *Emociones* (Emotions), considered to be one of his best to date. It surpassed record sales of his previous releases, selling close to 50,000 copies in Greece, 750,000 in Japan, and going double platinum (selling two million copies) in the Netherlands.

His accomplishment was staggering. Though a long list of European and Latin American artists have recorded very successfully in languages besides their own—Charles Aznavour, Abba, Enrico Macias, Luciano Pavarotti, Plácido Domingo, Roberto Carlos, José Luis Rodríquez, Camilo Sesto, Miguel Ríos, and many more—Julio is considered to be the most successful ever on the international level.

Partly, he's done this by making a point of feeling comfortable in each language he sings. Julio has often said that it's not the language you sing in, it's the way you present it. Something the French get excited over—a special inflection in your voice—may leave the Japanese completely cold or make them laugh hysterically.

He's not satisfied with correct pronunciation. To Julio Iglesias, the mood has to be conveyed, the feeling has to be there. A significant ingredient of his magic is this ability to convince listeners of his personal commitment to his every interpretation.

To the Frenchman, French is the language of love; to the Spaniard, love's language is Spanish; to the Italian, Italian; ad infinitum. As love's balladeer, Julio Iglesias has the good sense to reach the sensibilities where they live. In this, he's a master at playing the heartstrings. Even when his pronunciation falters, the empathy is there, and his listeners can't help but be truly touched by his efforts to sing in their native tongue.

In 1980, as the guest of President Anwar Sadat, Julio performed at the Pyramids of Egypt. At the invitation of Monaco's Princess Grace, he made a charity appearance at the 1980 Red Cross Ball. For a second time, he was invited to be one of the celebrity judges at the Miss Universe contest, this time held in New York City.

In these years, his name was often linked romantically with that of the beautiful and charming actress Sidney Rome. She had, said Julio, fascinating eyes. They seemed to be together as often as work permitted, traveling together when possible. One token of this media-covered romance was a dog that was brought to the U.S. from France aboard the Concorde. The Belgian Pointer was a gift from Sidney to Julio. He promptly christened it "Hey," after his hit song and album. Though the Sidney-Julio relationship eventually faded, the dog became a permanent resident in Julio's home.

For a fourth time, Julio went to the Viña del Mar song festival in Chile. While there, he became friendly with Priscilla Beaulieu Presley (best known then as the former wife of the late King of Rock, Elvis Presley; better known today, perhaps, as Jenna on TV's *Dallas*). Though they were frequently together, Julio adamantly denies that it was ever a serious romance.

His multilingual ascent to superstar heaven continued unabated in a number of languages, but English was not one of them. His U.S. penetration, though substantial, was still essentially to a Spanish-speaking public. However, things were happening in England. Vacationers to Europe were returning home with Julio's records. Word-of-mouth was spreading. Singing his own adaptation of Cole Porter's forty-year-old standard "Begin the Beguine"—a Spanish rendition with only the first words in English—Julio made waves. By late 1981, his version of "Begin the Beguine" was the number-one single in England. Both the single (over 500,000 copies) and the album (over 100,000 copies) went gold.

The year 1981, despite all the good luck it brought him, ended on a note of sheer terror for Julio. In December, his sixty-six-year-old father was kidnapped by Basque terrorists. The kidnappers demanded a $2,000,000 ransom. Advised not to pay, Julio and his family waited out the ordeal. Julio didn't go to Spain, for fear of attracting more attention to the incident, well aware that fanfare would only make matters worse. His brother, Carlos, was in Spain to do what had to be done, assisting the authorities in every possible way.

When the kidnappers could not be persuaded to give up their hostage, drastic measures were taken. On January 17, 1982, in the predawn darkness, Spanish antiterrorist forces descended on the house in the remote village of Trasmos, Spain, where Dr. Iglesias was imprisoned. Four of his captors were arrested and Dr. Iglesias, unharmed, was set free.

After Dr. Iglesias was released, he was flown to Miami. It was there that he was reunited with Julio. A press conference was held.

The Iglesias family had experienced, firsthand, the violent times in which we live. Reflecting on the horror of the kidnapping, and rejoicing in the outcome, Julio has since remarked that it could have turned out very differently. "I have seen the other side. I was joking and posing for pictures at [Egyptian President Anwar] Sadat's house just nine days before he was killed. Another nine days, who knows. I could have been with him."

Though Julio is remarkably philosophical today about both incidents, security for him and his family is very tight. The world being what it is, such measures have become a necessity, not a luxury, for the very famous and very rich.

Nineteen eighty-two brought more good fortune to Julio Iglesias as well.

Julio was familiar with Tony Renis's work before they got together to collaborate on the song "De Niña A Mujer" (From a Child to a Woman), dedicated to Julio's daughter, Chaveli. Julio wrote the lyrics, Renis the music. The two had known each other for two years and greatly respected each other's work when they met in Rome, while both were working on TV shows. Recalls Renis, "Julio was very *simpático*, remarkably accessible for someone who was an established superstar. He has an incredible personality."

"De Niña A Mujer" became a million-seller. In the Netherlands it went gold. In Japan it sold over 500,000 copies. In Brazil, it sold over two million.

In London, Julio performed at the prestigious Royal Albert Hall, scoring five sold-out nights. In Rio de Janeiro, Julio performed before an audience of 80,000 at the soccer stadium for the Flamengo team, wearing the team shirt on stage for part of the performance. In the United States, he performed at the Wolf Trap Theater in Virginia, before an audience that included Mrs. Ronald Reagan. In Paris, the Grevin Museum added a life-sized wax figure of Julio to their collection. CBS International awarded him the Crystal Globe, honoring him as their bestselling recording artist.

Julio and Diana Ross discussed the possibility of doing a song together, with Barry Gibb of the Bee Gees in mind as the producer. The plans, promising at the time, didn't materialize. However, Diana and Julio have since released the duet "All of You" and done a video by the same name. Says Diana of Julio, he's a rare performer with a gift of charisma "you can't do anything about."

*Momentos* was Julio's next album, produced by Ramón Arcusa. Julio and Tony Renis collaborated on the title song. The album became number one in country after country, leading one Spanish publication to single out Julio Iglesias as the "Figure of the Decade." In Japan alone, the album sold over 500,000 copies.

In 1982, Julio was already one of the Non-Japanese Big Five of the Japanese record market, ranking just behind Simon and Garfunkel, Olivia Newton-John, and Bertie Higgins, and just ahead of Billy Joel. Observes Bunny Freidus, vice president of creative operations for CBS Records International, "Traditionally, an artist singing in Spanish is rejected in France. A Spanish artist singing in French would be rejected by the snobby trend set." It was startling that Julio had no problems in France. But the icing on the cake was Japan. "I woke up to the fact that it was something different than normal when he broke in Japan. They can't even pronounce his name over there."

# TEN

# "AMERICA" DISCOVERS JULIO

*T*hough Julio Iglesias was already a star and a jet-setter in his own right, there were major constellations in Hollywood and New York in which he wasn't yet circulating. By 1982, even France was Julio's oyster. But the U.S., that elusive pearl, was still just beyond his grasp. Wrote Jon Marlowe of the *Miami News* in September 1982, "Most women don't even know his name, never mind scream it. But that may be changing." The occasion of this sage commentary was Julio's concert at the Miami Beach Theater of the Performing Arts.

Julio, not having performed in Miami for eighteen months, commanded his usual sold-out nights. He sang twenty-seven songs, and told the audience, "I will sing for you until I drop dead." He opened the show with "Quijote," from his *Momentos* album. When he sang "De Niña A Mujer," he brought his daughter, Chaveli, on stage, to be serenaded with the song written for her. When he asked the audience if they had to go to work the next day, they returned a vigorous "Noooo." He took encores. He stole hearts.

He entered 1983 with a better shot than ever at the English-speaking U.S. market. In his favor were all his previous supporters, along with a new one, the public relations firm of Rogers & Cowan. Rogers & Cowan, representatives of the likes of Paul McCartney, David Bowie, and Olivia Newton-John, were instrumental in the Julio Iglesias blitz that unfolded over the months that followed.

One of the first such arrangements made was Julio's appearance at the American Society of Technion's January 8, 1983, benefit for the Israel Institute of Technology. Julio was to be the "surprise" headline entertainer. The event, held at the Century Plaza in Los Angeles, was well attended by the movers and shakers of the West Coast.

Kirk Douglas was there to receive the A.S.T.'s Albert Einstein Award, to be presented by Burt Lancaster. It had been the idea of Kirk's Belgian-born wife, Anne, to invite Julio, whose work she was familiar with. Julio, always ready to listen to a request from a charitable organization, responded to the invitation with complete enthusiasm. Not only did he perform for free, but he put up a reported $60,000 of his own money to stage a show that included fifty musicians. The generous gesture and the superb show earned Julio a standing ovation.

In February, Julio appeared on Johnny Carson's "Tonight Show." Julio felt ill at ease in English. Johnny went out of his way to make him feel welcome and comfortable, expressing his admiration of Julio in Spanish.

In early March 1983, Julio played four nights at New York City's Radio City Music Hall. Already a fan, Gregory Peck was in the audience, cheering him on. Backed by a forty-piece orchestra, Julio sang in five languages. He received countless standing ovations, and gave encore after encore to his fans. One of his numbers, "As Time Goes By," was delivered in a not quite fluent English. But, reported *The New York Times,* "his debonair charm and splendidly virile singing made considerations of language almost irrelevant." After his Radio City debut, CBS Records Group President Walter Yetnicoff hosted a party for Julio at the swank Club A.

Julio was scheduled to appear in late March at the Universal Amphitheatre in Los Angeles (five sold-out performances). To thank him for his January A.S.T. benefit, Kirk and Anne Douglas threw a cocktail party for him at Chasen's. The tab ran high, and the guest list was dazzling. Among the glitterati were Joan Collins, Andy Williams, Gina Lollabrigida, Ursula Andress, Priscilla Presley, Charlton Heston, and Gregory Peck. The newspapers were quick to cover the event. So were the major TV news programs. So was "Entertainment Tonight."

As for the concert, but for one mishap, it would have been a perfect first night. Juggler-comic Michael Davis, opening the show for Julio, apparently destroyed his body mike while doing his stuff with a bowling ball. Nonetheless, his act was well received. As for Julio's performance, it won raves, with *Variety* finding him to be a crooner in the style of Perry Como, Andy Williams, and Johnny Mathis.

Bob Hope was eighty years old on March 29, 1983. His gala birthday special, attended by Bob Hope's friends President and Mrs. Ronald Reagan, Brooke Shields, Christie Brinkley, Tom Selleck, Cheryl Tiegs, and others, was held in Washington, D.C., and taped for television. Julio was one of the guests.

Nineteen eighty-three saw the domestic release of *Julio*. This album was a compilation of a series of previously published songs sung in English, Spanish, French, Italian, Portuguese, and German. CBS went all out to support the effort, spending a reported $300,000 to market it. The CBS sales force backed it strenuously. Julio plugged it on a second visit to "The Tonight Show."

Demand for the record was outstanding, not only in the strongly Spanish-speaking areas in the U.S., but in places like Arkansas, West Virginia, and Ohio. A Durham, North Carolina, record store buyer called Julio Iglesias "probably our number-one adult vocalist right now," and a Pittsburgh buyer observed, "Middle-aged women are going crazy over Iglesias' macho image."

Said *Variety*'s Richard Gold in a page-one story, "A little more than a month ago, NBC-TV comedian David Letterman was getting big laughs on his late-night show with a 'who's heard of

Julio Iglesias?' routine. But the last laugh has apparently gone to the handsome, Spanish international singing star." *Julio* was certified platinum, with record sales now over 1,000,000.

While making the movie "Romancing the Stone" in Mexico, actor-writer-producer Michael Douglas threw a party for Pedro Vargas. Vargas, one of the all-time most respected and loved balladeers of the Latin American market, had been helpful to Julio when the young singer was just starting out. In gratitude, Julio flew down to Michael's party to do honor to his old friend. It was a happy, heartwarming reunion. Mexico loved Julio all the more.

Despite Julio's unrelenting and successful advance on the American market, he continued to tour internationally. Though Julio hadn't made a major tour in Mexico in over four years, he followed in the footsteps of his colleague and compatriot Camilo Sesto, doing a benefit in Mexico City. He did a special on S.I.N. Mexican television, on the program "Siempre En Domingo" (Always on Sunday), with host Raúl Velasco. With him on the show was the great Pedro Vargas, who sang with Julio, making it a memorable and exciting occasion.

From Mexico to Japan is a major leap in both distances and cultures, yet Julio took the jump and landed firmly on his feet. Prior to his Japanese tour, CBS blitzed five of his albums there— *America, Por Una Mujer* (For a Woman), *Soy* (I Am), *A México* (To Mexico), and *A Flor de Piel* (Sensitive). They sold like hotcakes. Japan's fastest-selling album during the first six months of 1983 was Julio's *Momentos*. It outsold Japan's own super-hot Akina Nakamori's *Variations* by some 66,000 copies.

On a recent U.S. television show, Julio was asked to sing something in Japanese. He gave forth with a beautiful, lyrical, melodious few bars that elicited the response, "That's Spanish." Julio replied that no, it was Japanese—but the Japanese say the same thing when he sings in their tongue. Perhaps it's not the pronunciation but the thought that counts. In Julio's case, it counts to the tune of mighty millions in fans and record sales.

A series of concerts in May 1983 took Julio to Japan. The tour broke all previous records of any artists ever performing in Japan.

In August, he was touring Spain. Oddly enough, his popularity there had not been as sweeping as elsewhere in the world, essentially because, in the last years of Franco's government, protest songs were the ones in demand. But once back in Spain, the native son was welcomed with open arms. Noted *Variety*'s Madrid correspondent Peter Besas, "He has received voluble ovations everywhere he has appeared, as mobs of people, ranging from the humblest fans to Spanish royalty, have paid homage to the Spanish crooner."

Julio took his show to Palma de Mallorca, Málaga, La Coruña, Santander, Barcelona, and Madrid.

In Palma, he gave a gala benefit performance before King Juan Carlos de Borbon and Queen Sofia of Spain. It was his fourth visit with the royal family, as well as an opportunity to meet with the President of Spain's government, Felipe Gonzalez. In Barcelona's Camp Nou soccer stadium, he played to a crowd of over 60,000. The show was beautifully orchestrated. Julio gave the fans what they'd come for, and more.

Wrapping up his Spanish tour in Madrid, he performed at his former stomping grounds, Santiago Bernabeu Stadium, where, half a lifetime earlier, he'd played soccer for the Real Madrid team. He drew a standing-room-only crowd, close to 70,000. Only twice in the history of the stadium was it used for a nonsporting event. The second time was Julio's visit. The first was for the visit of Pope John Paul II.

For Julio, this was a tremendous, triumphal return to the land of his birth.

In late September, Julio celebrated his fortieth birthday, in Paris. In the late afternoon, at the palatial Hotel De Ville, Mayor Jacques Chirac of Paris presented Julio with the Medal of Honor of the City of Paris. He declared the day "Julio Iglesias Day." Later, Norris McWhirter, General Editor of the *Guinness Book of World Records,* bestowed on Julio their first-ever Diamond Disc Award for selling one hundred million albums, in seven languages worldwide.

CBS flew in celebrities, columnists, and record distributors from around the world. The lavish party was thrown at the Pré Catelan restaurant. Among the five hundred guests were Ursula Andress, Mirelle Methieu, longtime friend Regine, Donna Summer, Roman Polanski, and Leslie Caron. The champagne flowed, and Julio was beaming, surrounded by his friends and admirers.

Meanwhile, in London in 1983, Willie Nelson and his wife had heard Julio's "Begin the Beguine." It was the first time they'd heard him sing. Impressed by his vocal ability, Willie contacted CBS, their mutual label, when he returned to the States, and got Julio's phone number. He called Julio to say that he thought he was a great country singer.

Michael Davis, the juggler-comic who opens many of Julio's shows, makes this contribution to the background of that historic meeting: "I'm not saying I'm giving him comedy lessons, but he used to tell the story about going to meet Willie Nelson at his house and being greeted by this man at the gate wearing a beard and a bandana and thinking that was the porter. I told him Americans don't have porters, he should say 'I thought he was the gardener.' Now he gets a laugh."

The result of the meeting, the Julio-Willie duet "To All the Girls I've Loved Before," written by Albert Hammond and Hal David, opened new doors for Julio in the U.S. market. Willie Nelson fans who might never have thought twice about a Julio Iglesias record were suddenly discovering his voice. At the same time, the record served to introduce Willie Nelson to Julio's fans abroad.

Julio was Willie's guest at the 17th Annual Country Music Awards, where they sang the soon-to-be-released single. Before long, the song hit number one on *Billboard*'s Country Charts. In 1984, it won the Country Music Association Award for Vocal Duo of the Year.

Julio made his Atlantic City debut in November 1983, at the Superstar Theatre of Resorts International. He sold out the hall and delighted the critics, exuding, said one, "a wonderfully honest quality with a vague underlying sensuality. . . . The man and his music seem to blend into one."

In December 1983, he participated in the All-Star Party for Frank Sinatra, broadcast on national television. When Yuletide came, he was in Washington with President and Mrs. Ronald Reagan as one of the guest artists at the "Christmas in Washington" special done from the White House.

In February, Julio was at the Grammy Awards. There, with Melissa Manchester, he presented the award for Album of the Year to Michael Jackson.

In April, Julio was featured on both "On Stage America" and "20/20." On the first, a dramatization was presented of his soccer days, his accident, and his surgery. On that show, in an interview by Susie Coelho, Julio revealed that he'd promised himself he wouldn't stop—would not let himself die—until he'd had his opportunity to meet the American people. He said that, toward this end, he was working hours upon hours with his professor, Julie Adams, to perfect his pronunciation of the English language. On "20/20" he was interviewed by Barbara Walters. Again, he expressed his keen desire to conquer America.

In May, Julio flew to Madrid to receive one of the "Españoles de Nuestro Tiempo" (Spaniards of our Times) awards from the Spanish publication El Tiempo. Among the other recipients was the Spanish Defense Minister, Narciso Serra.

His single with country great Willie Nelson, "To All the Girls I've Loved Before," was getting play on the country stations and pop stations too. It climbed on both charts, reaching the number-one slot on the country charts for two consecutive weeks, and reaching as high as number-five on the pops. "To All the Girls I've Loved Before" topped a million sales, earning for both Julio and Willie another gold record. At the same time, it was also making the charts abroad.

Julio, meanwhile, was busily assembling the components of his first aimed-at-the-U.S. album, *1100 Bel Air Place,* and the single "All of You" with Diana Ross.

Ramón Arcusa, Julio's longtime producer, was present for the initial *1100 Bel Air Place* meetings between Julio and American record producer Richard Perry. These had occurred in 1983, when the idea had been to generate a new sound for Julio, more American, more pop-oriented. But there were delays, details to be ironed out, decisions to be made. One of the decisions concerned how radical a change Julio would make in his style.

During this period of delay, the *Julio* album had been released, capitalizing on the enthusiasm that had been building for a U.S. album by the artist, and also paving the way for *1100 Bel Air Place*. With the tremendous success of *Julio* it became clear that Julio Iglesias wouldn't have to make much of a *volte face* to score in this country. The same style that scored time after time in Chile, in Japan, in Mexico, in France, in the Netherlands, and elsewhere on several continents, had demonstrably won over much of the U.S. record-buying public. It no longer seemed necessary for Julio to be anyone but himself.

The album *1100 Bel Air Place* was to have been produced entirely by Richard Perry, who has worked with such talents as the Pointer Sisters, Art Garfunkel, Manhattan Transfer, Carly Simon, and Diana Ross. Perry felt it would be wise to include Albert Hammond in the proceedings, not only because of his musical talents, but because of Hammond's excellent command of both English and Spanish. Besides being associate producer of the album, Hammond wrote the music for "To All the Girls I've Loved Before," with lyrics by Hal David; the English lyrics for "Me Va, Me Va" (It Goes Well With Me); music and lyrics for "Moonlight Lady" along with Carole Bayer Sager; music and lyrics from "Bambou Medley" (song: "Jamaica") along with Julio and Michel Colombier; and the music and lyrics for "The Air That I Breathe" along with Michael Hazlewood.

Gradually, Ramón Arcusa added his active assistance to the production of the album. With all these distinguished contributors, and with arrangements by John Barnes, Tony Renis, Michel Colombier, Robbie Buchanan, Ramón Arcusa, Randy Kerber, Nicky Hopkins, and Paulinho Da Costa, the album had "chartbuster" written all over it.

Yet when all the components were finally together and the record was ready to go to press—Julio stopped the presses! He still wasn't 100 percent satisfied with the mix, and insisted that changes be made. No wonder Julio has referred to this as probably the most expensive album in history.

The changes were made, with spectacular results. *1100 Bel Air Place,* named for the Los Angeles address where Julio lived while making the record, immediately hit the charts.

Two duets from the album—"To All the Girls I've Loved Before" with Willie Nelson, and "All of You" with Diana Ross—would lend new dimensions to the notion of Julio Iglesias as a crossover artist. Julio's voice would be heard on radio programs, TV shows, and turntables that never before had played him.

Concurrently, he'd be appearing in concert halls, stadiums, clubs, and theaters in cities he'd never before seen. These would be U.S. cities. Cities clamoring for Iglesias. At last.

Julio's moment had arrived.

# HARD WORK
# AND SUCCESS

Manolo

Manolo

Manolo

*The Olympia Theatre in Paris (opposite page). Olympia Theatre where he recorded his first live album (top). From his first film, "La Vida Sigue Igual" (above). With mike in hand ready to caress a melody (left).*

Danny Feld/Shooting Star

Elizabeth Garcia

*H*ey is introduced to Susie
Coelho from "On Stage America"
(above). During his performance at
Resorts International in Atlantic
City (right).

*Danny Feld/Shooting Star*

*J*ulio enjoying a good laugh during interview (left). Performing at the prestigious Florida Park Club in Madrid, 1977 (below). Julio in concert (bottom).

*Manolo*

*Anastasia Fantsios/Star File*

*T*he many emotions of Julio (below). At the
Israel Institute of Technology's Albert Einstein
Awards Dinner for Kirk Douglas, where Julio
was a special performer (right). With Susie
Coelho during the interview for "On Stage
America" (bottom).

Anastasia Pantsios/Star File

Peter C. Borsari

Danny Feld/Shooting Star

Manolo

*Never one to play to a small crowd (top). With Brazilian soccer great Pele (above right). Julio and Luis De Carlos, President of the Real Madrid soccer team (above left).*

Manolo

Manolo

*P*osing with musicians after a recording session. Far left, Manuel de la Calva, and kneeling, Julio's producer Ramón Arcusa (top). At the Benidorm Song Festival where his work was introduced (left). "El Dúo Dinámico", Manuel de la Calva, Ramón Arcusa and Julio in the control room during a recording session (below).

Manolo

*A*lways with a smile on his lips and in his eyes (right). At his old stomping ground, Bernabeu Stadium, showing us he hasn't lost his touch (below and below right).

Danny Feld/Shooting Star

Manolo

Manolo

*B*elting out a song in concert (right). Which language should I record in next (middle)? Outside his Bel Air home where he recorded "1100 Bel Air Place" (bottom).

Anastasia Pantsios/Star File

Fotos International/Pictorial Parade, Inc.

H. Gallo/Shooting Star

Manolo

Elizabeth García

Juan Rivera

*J*ulio with a small part of his gold record collection, (395 to date...) (top right). Singing "Never, Never, Never" with Janey Clewer at Resorts International (above left). With Bob Hope and Coca-Cola President Donald Keough (left).

# ELEVEN

# TOUR '84

Backed by a concerted media blitz," wrote Paul Grein in a July 1984 issue of *The Los Angeles Times,* "Julio Iglesias has become America's latest instant celebrity."

As incredible as it may seem, after all the work and huge international success, in the eyes of most of the U.S. public, Julio simply appeared overnight. The majority of the U.S. population was asleep to any thought of Julio. Only Julio Iglesias had been viligant and awake—just like Don Quijote the night before undertaking his glorious quest. Just as a knight of old kept vigil in preparation for the moment when he went forth to conquer, Julio waited and kept watch. When the moment was right, he entered the fray, armed with the lance of Coca-Cola.

It was the deftest stroke yet in his brilliantly crafted strategy to conquer the U.S. market.

On May 2, 1984, the world or close to it (about ninety countries, representing 80 percent of the world's population) received live, by satellite broadcast, "a press conference to remember." It was held in the Astor Room of the Waldorf-Astoria in New York City. Donald Keough, President of Coca-Cola, announced the signing of a three-year contract with Julio Iglesias. The contract specified that Julio would promote the soft drink through print, radio, and television. In return, Coca-Cola would sponsor his concert tour for the next three years, beginning with a seven-month, fifty-city tour over six continents. It would kick off in the summer of 1984 in the United States and Canada.

Since Coca-Cola is one of the founding sponsors of the Statue of Liberty–Ellis Island Centennial Campaign, Julio also agreed to active involvement in charity concerts and fundraising dinners to benefit the Centennial restoration. Given his sincere admiration for the principles represented by the Statue of Liberty, and his appeal to audiences in six languages, it was a responsibility he was more than happy to take on. Speaking at the press conference, he commented, "Being European and Latin, I can especially appreciate what the Statue of Liberty symbolizes to the world . . . brotherhood and the spirit of friendship among nations . . . She is one of the girls I've loved before."

Also gracing the press conference was campaign chairman Bob Hope. It was a reunion of sorts for Bob and Julio, since Julio had participated in Bob's Washington D.C. birthday celebration along with a long list of other performers and V.I.P.'s.

Not disclosed at the press conference were the exact financial details of the arrangement. However, the value of the package is rumored to be between $5,000,000 and $20,000,000.

Exact figures aside, the Coca-Cola contract was, for Julio, the perfect move to get him out in front of all the U.S.A. For Coca-Cola, it was a terrific opportunity to expand their market on a worldwide scale.

The impact of the move—which expressed itself largely in an extensive crosscountry Coca-Cola-sponsored tour for Julio—was monumental. Julio played to sell-out crowds from Los Angeles to New York City and points in between.

To people who hadn't witnessed the Julio Iglesias phenomenon years earlier in Europe, in Central or South America, in Japan, or even in New York's Madison Square Garden in 1976, it *appeared* to be overnight. But now, for Julio, the long night was over. It was time to wake up and live his impossible dream.

At the beginning of 1984, what was true of Julio's music was perhaps even more true of his live performances: the U.S. market was a tough nut to crack. And though a Spanish publication named him "Figure of the Decade," he was still pretty much "Julio who?" in the country he most wanted to conquer.

Moreover, though Julio was finally prepared to surmount it, the language barrier was still very real. It had been real for the Swedish group Abba in the 1970s, a group with worldwide record sales comparable to the Beatles, but without the natural ease in English to overcome public resistance. It's been real for Demis Roussos and Nana Mouskouri, international megastars who have yet to hit big in the United States.

It has, therefore, been a very real necessity for Julio Iglesias to become comfortable enough in the English language not only to sing, but also to manage the patter that goes with a live show. On his 1984 U.S. tour, he sang in English, French, Spanish, and Italian. He spoke in English. Bill Kaufman of Long Island, New York's *Newsday* called his the "hottest voice fracturing English these days," but the fact is that Julio scarcely bruised the language. To the contrary, Julio's new, improved English—about which he joked during his performances—seems to have entirely met the need.

Of course, it wasn't enough merely for Julio Iglesias to sharpen his English in order to go on stage and sing. He needed songs, and for this tour he chose a repertoire that included "Begin the Beguine," "As Time Goes By," "Cucurucucu Paloma," "When I Fall in Love," "Moonlight Lady," "Hey," "Canto a Galicia," "Me Va, Me Va," "Vaya Con Dios," "La Mer," "La Vie En Rose," "To All The Girls I've Loved Before," "Amor," and "Abrázame" (with Italian lyrics).

Along with the songs and the patter, he needed a fully staged show. In this, he worked with Joe Layton. The result was an arrangement of moving video screens, a multilevel moving mini-amphitheater on which the orchestra sat, and a screen that wrapped around the back of the stage to take projected images of moonlit stars, space, and clouds. The moving video screens were used for projected images of Julio himself, allowing him to sing duets with himself or, when singing "To All the Girls I've Loved Before," with himself dressed to look like Willie Nelson.

Backing up Julio on stage was an orchestra of varying sizes depending on the size of the house, with saxophone soloist J.A. Granata and very talented female vocalists Janey Clewer, Stephanie Spruill, and Pamela Bunning. Granata contributed the sax solo in Julio's rendition of "When I Fall In Love" (played by Stan Getz on Julio's recording of the song). Stephanie Spruill joined Julio in a stunning duet of "As Time Goes By," and Janey Clewer sang with him the haunting "Never, Never, Never."

Opening the show was juggler-comic Michael Davis, who had the difficult task of warming up the audience while quieting it down. To do this, he told jokes, played the guitar, sang funny, and juggled a bowling ball, an egg, and frighteningly sharp objects. People laughed, enjoyed, applauded . . . and waited anxiously for Julio to come out on stage.

When Michael Davis left and Julio entered, the crowd invariably went wild. Often, they had to wait a long while between Michael Davis's exit and Julio's first step on stage. The longer they waited, the greater the tension that built in the audience. The greater the tension, the more explosive was the burst of applause that greeted his appearance.

There stood Julio—"not androgynous like Michael Jackson . . . neither is he aggressively masculine like Tom Jones," according to a recent *Time* article, but "the elegant male, well dressed and sophisticated, but with a boyish, ingratiating smile." He looked *macho*, not in the way that the term is overused today, but in the romantic, old-fashioned Spanish sense. Not like a mule driver, like an exceptionally charming man.

Though he spoke to his audience primarily in English, at some shows, he asked, in Spanish, How many of *mi gente* (my people) are here tonight? Some reviewers have taken *mi gente* to refer to his fans, but since he asked the question in Spanish, the meaning is quite clearly "How many fellow Latins are here tonight?" The audience response to this question was never less than resounding.

Describing Julio's audience, Michael Davis explained to one reporter, "Julio's a romantic idol. . . . Certain parts of his audience are made up of fans who've loved him for years, and they're Spanish, Europeans, South Americans, everything but your average Middle American. This isn't a rock audience. It's pretty upper crust. They get dressed up when they go out."

His audience was that. Soon, it was more. Soon it included the average Middle American in great numbers. And in some cities, it included people who didn't get dressed up when they went out.

It included men, as well as women, who liked what they heard. Most applauded enthusiastically, some bellowed their enthusiasm, and a number of women noisily swooned. The recently converted Julio fans were there, along with the longtime loyal supporters, in abundance.

How loyal are Julio's fans? One became so incensed when *New York Daily News* columnist Liz Smith wrote negatively of Julio, that the fan subsequently wrote Ms. Smith that she'd never again buy the *Daily News*.

Yes, there stood Julio on stage—with his songs, with his show, with his loyal fans—in Denver, in Los Angeles, in Toronto, in New York, in Hartford, in Atlantic City, in U.S. cities from east to west, from north to south. Julio—The Conqueror!

On the night of June 21, 1984, Julio appeared on "The Tonight Show" with his good friend and great booster, host Johnny Carson. Julio spoke about his records, his upcoming tour, and his difficulty in learning English. "Girls," he said, was the hardest word he had to learn, yet one of the words he had the most use for. Now, smiled Julio, he no longer says "Gerlsz" but "Gur-ur-urls."

When Johnny asked if Julio had any difficulty communicating with U.S. women, Julio answered, with an ingratiating smile, that he had problems with the lyrics, but not with his hands.

After singing a song and relating a few anecdotes, Julio let the audience in on a big secret. None other than Willie Nelson just

happened to be backstage, to sing with Julio their crossover su-
perhit duet, "To All the Girls I've Loved Before." Julio then
strode to center-stage position. From behind the curtain came the
familiar bandana-wearing figure of Willie Nelson—but it wasn't
Willie Nelson at all. It was Johnny Carson, looking and singing
enough like Nelson to be his clone. It was clever. It was funny.
Most importantly, it showed that Julio had a sense of humor that
could cross over as easily as his music.

Julio Iglesias kicked off his first U.S. tour at the foot of the
Rocky Mountains in Denver, Colorado, on June 22, 1984. The
concert grossed $138,444. The crowd totaled nearly 10,000. The
date was declared, by Denver's Hispanic mayor Federico Pena,
"Julio Iglesias Day."

The setting was the Red Rock Amphitheater, an outdoor facility
so beautifully situated that Julio was enchanted by the surround-
ings, and interrupted several of his songs to comment on them.
Throughout the evening, he stopped to talk to the audience, accepting their offers of roses and kissing their children.

For one song, "When I Fall In Love," he had to read the English
lyrics, telling the audience, "This is the first concert I do in my
life with so many Saxon people."

For another, "To All the Girls I've Loved Before," he told the
audience what had happened on "The Tonight Show" the previous evening. He went on to say that Johnny Carson was in the
area and might have it in mind to come on stage, to repeat his
clone-of-Willie-Nelson duet with Julio. With this, a bandana-
wearing figure appeared onstage, and the crowd clamored chants
of "Johnny, Johnny, Johnny" as they rose to their feet to
see . . . the legendary Willie Nelson! For the second time in two
nights, Iglesias had put one over on an American audience. His
fans loved it. The duet with Willie Nelson was an extra added
attraction. But with or without Nelson, it was Julio Iglesias'
Day—and Night.

From Denver, Julio worked his way south and west: The Tin-
gley in Albuquerque, Celebrity Theater in Phoenix, and Caesar's
Palace at Lake Tahoe.

On July Fourth, he joined the rest of the United States on the 208th Anniversary of their Independence by taking time out of his hectic schedule to fly out to Washington, D.C. The site of the extravaganza was the Washington Monument. There, with the Beach Boys, he sang "The Air That I Breathe" (which he also sings with them on his album *1100 Bel Air Place*). He also sang, with lyric in hand, a song with LaToya Jackson, one of Michael Jackson's younger sisters. Former Beatle Ringo Starr was among the event's headliners. The cheering audience neared 400,000.

From Washington, he headed west again, to Las Vegas. He played the fabulous MGM Grand, his third time there. Said *Variety* of this point in his career, "Julio Iglesias is no longer the simple multi-millionaire of the multi-million record sales" but now "a world-class star" in a show "in keeping with the multi-million-billion effect."

From Las Vegas on to another appearance on Johnny Carson's show, and to the Pan American Center in Las Cruces, New Mexico, then The Summit in Houston, the Dallas Convention Center in Dallas, the World Expo in New Orleans, the Greek Theater in San Francisco, and Los Angeles, Julio kept moving. In March of 1983, he'd sold out five performances in L.A.'s immense Universal Amphitheater.

This time, during the Summer Olympics—even with the likes of Joan Baez, Diana Ross, Linda Ronstadt, and Juice Newton slated for the next few weeks at the Amphitheater—he sold out an unprecedented ten nights, which grossed $1,700,000. Because of his enormous popularity abroad, tickets to the concerts had been included in a number of the tour packages offered to visitors coming to the U.S. for the Olympic Games. It was another example of the ingenious sort of marketing foresight we've come to associate with Julio Iglesias. The success of this idea is particularly striking when you remember that his first album aimed specifically at the U.S. market, *1100 Bel Air Place*, hadn't even been released yet.

For an added attraction at this opening night with a $250-a-seat orchestra section, Julio premiered the video made with Diana Ross of their hit duet, "All of You." Reviewer Paul Grein found the video, as well as the rest of the show, stiff and reserved, calling Julio a "low-voltage performer." Noting that Julio was still in the early stages of his tour, he suggested that Julio "loosen up." He also commented favorably on the American standards Julio sang, and wished he'd sing more.

Perhaps—as people watching the progress of the tour at early stages as well as later ones have remarked—Julio wasn't being stiff, reserved, low voltage, or uptight. He was simply dead on his feet. The pace of the tour was grueling from start to finish. There were weeks on end when he performed in a different city every night. In quite a few of these cities, there were parties thrown in his honor *after* the performances—a tremendous honor, but also a tremendous drain on stamina.

Los Angeles was just such a case. On this particular evening, the post-concert dinner, held at the Sheraton Premiere Hotel, was attended by celebrities like George Segal, Peter Falk, Dionne Warwick, and Angie Dickinson. Julio was expected to arrive around 11:00 P.M. He didn't arrive until after 1:00 in the morning, escorting Brooke Shields. By then, many of the guests, without a clue as to when the guest of honor would appear, had departed. Some had simply been too tired to stay any later. Julio, on the other hand, having given a long, exhausting concert, seemed perhaps too tired to have come any earlier. Yet the tour had barely begun.

From Los Angeles, he went on to the State Fair Grounds in Milwaukee, Pine Knob in Detroit, the Mann Music Center in Philadelphia, Boston Common in Boston, The Forum in Montreal, and Toronto. In Toronto, he was a headlining attraction at the world's biggest annual fair, the CNE, the Canadian National Exhibition or "The Ex."

The Ex, in its 106th year, ran twenty days in late August and early September 1984. It covered 350 acres along Toronto's waterfront on Lake Ontario. It celebrated Toronto's 150th birthday, Ontario's 200th birthday, the 75th anniversary of powered flight in Canada, and the 60th anniversary of the Royal Canadian Air Force. It offered a midway complete with barkers and games of chance; carnival rides and circus candy; trick water skiing and water ballet accompanied by lights, special effects, and music; a Celebrity Hog-Calling Contest; a Miss CNE–Queen of the Fair pageant; an Amateur Bodybuilding Competition; the 78th Annual Royal Canadian Cat Club Championship; and the 35th Canadian International Air Show.

In short, the CNE was spectacular, and so were the stellar performers appearing in the Grandstand Concert Series as part of the festivities. To name a few: Frank Zappa performed on August fifteenth, Julio Iglesias on the sixteenth, The Beach Boys on the twentieth, Willie Nelson on the twenty-seventh, Rod Stewart on the thirtieth, and Frank Sinatra on September second. The CNE was an entertainment extravaganza.

Julio's performance sold out.

The 1984 reaction to Julio in Canada was much the same as the 1984 U.S. reaction. While many people were going along saying "Julio who?" plenty of fans had gone to tremendous lengths to see his show. A couple of fans drove through fog and rain, arriving at 5:00 A.M. to be first at the CNE box office when the Julio tickets went on sale. They waited what seemed to be a cold, damp eternity on line. When the box office opened, they discovered that all floor seats and center bleachers had been reserved for V.I.P.'s. The best they could get was seats in the twenty-fourth row. When the tickets all sold and the smoke had cleared, no one was saying "Julio who?" any longer.

Close to 25,000 fans attended the Toronto concert.

Noting the ethnic mix of the audience (primarily English, French, Spanish, and Italian), reviewer Liam Lacey remarked in Toronto's *Globe and Mail*: "The odds were good that at any given point in last night's show, at least a third of the audience had no idea what he was singing about." But the other side of the coin is that *at least* they all understood him at some point—something that can be said for few performers when the audience is as ethnically varied. Besides, as many a reviewer has said of Julio in years past, and no doubt will say in years to come, his music transcends language. He doesn't need an interpreter to get his message across.

Throughout the evening, Julio was exciting, charming, and self-effacing, even to admitting that the first time he visited Toronto, "nobody came." The stoniest heart would have had to admit that romance filled the air. "What a man. What a ham. What a show," Liam Lacey concluded.

And while Julio's first visit to Toronto may have left something to be desired, this time certainly made up for it in terms of visibility. More than once, *The Toronto Star* reported his pre- and post-concert personal arrangements. One headline story reported that a special clause in Julio's contract called for caviar (Beluga) and wine ($60 a bottle) prior to his performance. Another headlined the story, "Julio takes the Mayfair suite at posh Sutton Place Hotel." The suite, according to the article, was the same one used by Mary Tyler Moore when filming a TV movie earlier in the year; the hotel was the same one used by Tom Bosley when he filmed a garbage-bag commercial in Toronto.

Julio followed up Toronto with performances at The Central Canadian Exposition in Ottawa and the Blossom Music Center in Cleveland.

"A year ago," Julio told a reporter, "someone asked me when I would consider myself a success in America. I told him I'd be happy the day I put 10,000 people together in Ohio. In Cleveland, I got nearly 20,000." Julio was happy in his success. The audience was ecstatic over Julio.

From Cleveland, he headed for the Performing Arts Center in Saratoga, The Rosemont in Chicago, the State Fair Grounds in Minneapolis, the State Fair Grounds in Syracuse, and the Jones Beach Theater on Long Island in New York.

The Jones Beach Theater in 1984 was voted the best outdoor facility in the country by readers of *Performance Magazine,* a trade journal of the music and concert business. Built right on the water, it had been a long-time stronghold of musical comedy. But in recent years, *West Side Story* and *Damn Yankees* simply weren't filling enough seats, and so a dramatic change was made. Top acts were brought in, among them Peter Allen, The Moody Blues, The Thompson Twins, James Taylor and Randy Newman, The Association and Three Dog Night, Frank Zappa, Crosby, Stills & Nash, The Beach Boys, Rod Stewart, and Julio Iglesias. Once again, Julio Iglesias sold out—in one day.

The evening of the performance came. Storm clouds darkened the sky over the outdoor theater, threatening to deprive the fans of even a glimpse of the superstar. Crowds expectantly lined up to enter the theater. A few clustered at the stage entrance, hoping to spot or talk to Julio. When show time approached and fans hadn't seen him, there was some concern that he might have gotten caught in traffic. But then his voice was heard piercing the air, coming from inside the theater, as he finished up rehearsals.

The show started, more punctually than usual, very shortly after 8:00 P.M. Because rain was expected at any minute, Michael Davis didn't go on, and Julio opened for himself. The crowd was delighted—and Julio had an object lesson in what it means to be an opening act. Latecomers filed into their seats in droves. They were noisy, and so was the wind whipping at Julio on stage. At one point, Julio was so bothered by the disruptions, he commented to the audience, "This is the first time in the United States that I see so many people moving."

Yet once the audience was seated, Julio was at top form. He was relaxed. There was no sign that the ordeal of the tour was taking its toll. People who had followed his career for years said they never saw him so comfortable with his audience, so in his element. Everything—including the fresh sea air that assaulted him—seemed to agree with Julio.

He opened the show with Cole Porter's haunting "Begin the Beguine," interrupting it to remark, "The wind is so hard I'm going to fly." He continued to interrupt himself throughout the evening, commenting, kidding, relating how hard it was for him to learn English. He explained that he used to call his toes "fingers" because the word that means *toes* in Spanish means *fingers* too. He joked about life, about love, about sex. "The last time I kiss an American I get pregnant," he said.

"I get boring on stage if I don't have fun myself," said Julio. He seemed to be having as much fun as his most ardent fans.

His fans showered him with flowers and balloons, and from one member of the audience he received a Spanish flag. Accepting the flag, he kissed it and said, "I love you." One moment he was praising Spain, at another, the U.S.A. "I'm in love with this country. I want to die in the United States." He said it was wonderful that these are *united states*, and not many tiny, separate countries. His sincerity was beyond question, reflecting his "dual citizenship of the spirit" with Spain and the United States.

Toward the end of the concert, he learned that the latecomers who had been so distracting earlier in the evening were not to blame. Traffic had been unusually heavy. When he returned to the stage, he apologized to them, dedicating his next song to "the thousand people who came late because of traffic."

Julio's closing received a standing ovation. He returned the compliment by asking the audience to join him in a few choruses of "Vaya Con Dios." The harmony was commendable, so good it might have been rehearsed. The evening ended on an exhilarating note. And not a drop of rain fell until several hours after the show's end.

From Jones Beach Julio dashed off to Merriweather Post Pavilion in Baltimore, the Concord in New York's Catskill Mountains, Carnegie Music Hall in Pittsburgh, the Kennedy Center in Washington, D.C., and was back in New York for a week-long engagement at Radio City Music Hall beginning September 6.

His arrival in New York City was feted with a party at Regine's. Guests included Hugh O'Brian, New York State Governor and Mrs. Hugh Carey, Alexander Godunov, the Arthur Ashes, Cornelia Guest, Harry Reasoner, and other top celebrities. When one pushy character asked Julio, "What have you got that I haven't got," Julio returned, "The ability to survive." He more than survived. He surpassed. He also sang, to Regine, her favorite Julio song, "Me Va, Me Va." Another party, given by CBS Records at Windows on the World atop the World Trade Center, added to the merriment.

When the Radio City tickets went on sale, the line went around the block—a very long city block. A million dollars worth of tickets sold in the next fifteen hours. Those on line showed not only extreme loyalty but in some instances blind loyalty, because there were people waiting on line who had never heard Julio Iglesias sing. Some had been standing since the crack of dawn on the strength of word-of-mouth recommendations. One woman had seen him on "The Today Show" and was so impressed with the way he expressed himself that she wanted to see him in person. She was willing to stand on line, no matter how long it took. Others on line had come because they were familiar with his Willie Nelson duet, "To All the Girls I've Loved Before."

Some people had taken off from work or school just to stand on line. Others, mostly Spanish-speaking, older people—an unusual group to be found waiting on line for concert tickets—stood their ground. As the long wait wore on, one man made a phone call for another who asked him to "tell my family where I am."

Opening night was an Event with a capital E. Limousines of all sizes and colors surrounded the Music Hall, as did Rolls Royces and a horse-drawn carriage. There were klieg lights, TV camera crews, ticket scalpers, and souvenir hawkers galore. As women entered the theater, they were given long-stemmed roses, compliments of Julio, Coca-Cola, and WYNY radio.

Once more, Michael Davis opened, joking that Julio Iglesias was the father of all the Menudos. Once more, the audience was patiently amused, but full of anticipation for what was to come.

Julio came out, looking tired, even nervous, but quite splendid nonetheless. More comfortable with English than he'd been in previous years—more comfortable than he'd been, in fact, at the start of the tour—he told the audience how much easier it was for him now to be able to interpret the songs with feeling, to give them the right shadings and nuances, since he fully understood what he was singing.

In the audience were New York mayor Ed Koch and the fabulous Diana Ross. Diana, who had recorded the hit single "All of You" with Julio, was urged by the crowd to get up on stage. A screening of the "All of You" video with Diana served to intensify their eagerness. Constant cries of "We love you, Diana," finally got her up there beside Julio, but she didn't sing. She kissed him, and mentioned her upcoming concert at Radio City Music Hall (which was to sell out eleven performances in a matter of hours).

As in the past, audience members came to the stage with kisses, flowers and—again—one person gave him a Spanish flag, which he fondly embraced.

The September 10 Radio City performance was a benefit for Casita María, the first settlement house in New York City to serve the needs of the Hispanic community. Founded in 1934, Casita María chose this occasion to mark fifty years of programs in the arts, athletics, education, nutrition, and mental health for the people it serves. The concert, combined with a Casita María supper dance at the Plaza Hotel, raised $250,000 for the cause. Casita María presented Julio with a gold medal. Accepting it graciously, Julio promised to come back for future benefits.

On closing night at Radio City Music Hall, the audience was a demanding "Julio crowd." They were so demanding, in fact, that some voiced their frustrations when he played too much to one side of the house or the other. At one point, he walked over to the left side of the stage. A fan sitting at the far right called to him to come sit on the right for a while. Julio replied, "Don't they know that when they do that, they make me go farther away?" At this, some members of the audience mumbled "Wrong move—at $30 a ticket" and walked even farther away than Julio; they left the theater.

Also that evening, a little girl came up to the foot of the stage to hand Julio flowers. Julio brought her up on stage to sit next to him. In speaking to her, he found out that her parents were Latin but hadn't taught her to speak Spanish. He proceeded to bring her mother on stage, to stress the importance of knowing both languages, and passing along a twin heritage. At the same time, he praised the U.S. for being a country where children can assimilate so quickly. He also suggested orthodonture for the little girl!

Unintentionally, these actions offended a few fans, who took their grievances to the letter columns in one or two New York papers. One letter writer expressed annoyance that Julio chastised the mother. The mother, Connie Espinoza, sent the paper her reply. She wrote that she would not criticize Julio's comments and had in fact taken them constructively. She added that she and her daughter will always remember sharing the stage with Julio, particularly when he sang "When I Fall in Love" to her daughter.

With a few exceptions, the closing night audience seemed wildly enamored of Julio Iglesias. They hated to see him leave, but he had to tear himself away. There was to be, after all, a ninetieth-anniversary celebration for the music and record industry "bible" Billboard, to be held at Studio 54, featuring Julio as the main guest. He arrived at Studio 54 later than expected, and was unable to stay more than a few minutes. However, he remained long enough to have a piece of birthday cake on stage and sing "Happy Birthday" to Billboard.

From Radio City and Studio 54 he went on to Hartford, Connecticut, and the sizable Civic Center. For this concert, tickets had sold out twice—once when they first went on sale, and again when new seats were made available by a change in the stage design to accomodate more fans.

In the audience was an American mother of three who had first heard of him while vacationing in Melbourne, Australia. Already she owned five of the artist's records, and was busily tracking down a sixth. She'd paid over $100 to attend the concert with her children, and thought Julio had the magnetic power of Tom Jones, Tom Selleck, and Neil Diamond rolled into one.

From the audience, a fan came up to kiss him. He knelt down to her, remarking, "Only in America can I do this with the boyfriend right here. In my country never. The boyfriend kills you. Here it's wonderful." He also said. "Your boyfriend loves you. I know this because I know you said to him, 'You don't take me to see Iglesias, you don't love me at all.'"

The Hartford crowd was a huge one—13,000—in an almost cavernous hall. Visibility wasn't terrific from some seats, nor were acoustics always perfect. As a result, one fan called out "Julio, no se oye nada" (Julio, no one can hear anything). The truth is that acoustics were fine, if echoey, when he sang, but muffled at times when he spoke. The truth may also be that it's hard for a singer onstage to imagine what it's like for a fan way up in a bleacher, straining to hear over row upon row of audience noises.

The truth, too, is that a few small contingents in the Hartford crowd were so boisterously appreciative that it was no doubt impossible for Julio to know the rude fans from the rest. There were some in limited-visibility seats yelling so loudly, "Julio, come here where I can see you," that people sitting around them could neither see nor hear Julio Iglesias. This provided another glimpse of Julio's traditional Spanish *macho* approach to women. His reaction was to ignore the ones who bellowed incessantly at the tops of their lungs. Indeed, it's not in the *macho* tradition to sing a love song to a woman who behaves like a bouncer in a cheap dive. However, when these women quieted down, Julio was quick to come around to their side of the stage to serenade them.

From Hartford, it was on to Resorts International in Atlantic City, with hardly enough time between to catch a breath.

Resorts International, the first hotel/casino to open in Atlantic City, just happens to house the largest theater in Atlantic City, the Superstar Theater. The resort holds the record for big-ticket affairs, for instance Luciano Pavarotti's premiere casino appearance in 1983, at which the cheapest tickets went for $200.

Julio had first appeared in Atlantic City in November 1983. His initial success there no doubt contributed to the speed of ticket sales in 1984, selling out nine shows over a seven-night period, for a theater with a seating capacity of 1700.

Reported Jerry Blavat in the Atlantic City show column "Geator Gab," "Tickets went on sale and were guzzled up immediately; not since the early days of Sinatra has such a pandemonium developed over at Resorts."

The press conference preceding Julio's opening night performance at Resorts started "a tad" late, causing some journalists to wonder about the beautiful collection of watches—over forty— that Julio Iglesias is reputed to have but rarely wears. Observed Atlantic City *Press* reviewer David J. Spatz, "Using the Iglesias Time Conversion Factor, one tad equals two and a half hours." One photographer was heard to mutter about the "luxuries of superstardom—to own a watch you never have to look at."

The Resorts audience was not a typical concert crowd. Indeed, Resorts International's Superstar Theater isn't a concert hall. It's a nightclub. At one midnight show, a voice in the crowd kept hammering at Julio to sing "Cumbia"—a Colombian dance music totally unrelated to Julio's style or repertoire.

Julio, who by now had been plugging away at his tour for nearly three months, did his best to ignore the voice. But what he couldn't ignore was an estranged couple arguing during one of his love ballads. The woman, it seems, had spotted her husband with another woman. She threw a drink at him. The husband retaliated by decking her with one punch. Julio tried to calm them down, without success. His efforts not only failed to quiet the couple, they also provoked one heckler to snap, "Go back to Spain." The commotion just about drowned out Julio's song. Security guards had to escort the pair from the club.

Fortunately, Julio didn't lose his momentum. He delivered a throughly professional, stylish show, which was highlighted when the casino surprised him with a giant girl-filled birthday cake to celebrate his forty-first.

Two nights after the opening, a star-studded list of jet-setters descended on Atlantic City "to share an evening of thrill and romance with Julio Iglesias." Regine, along with James Crosby, Chairman of the Board of Resorts International, hosted the event, which consisted of cocktails, the show, and an international buffet supper of specialty foods from around the world. The guests came by plane, by helicopter, and by limousine. They included Bella Abzug, Gael Greene, Barbara Howar, Irving "Swifty" Lazar, Guy Laroche, Mary McFadden, Count Rudy Crespi, Baroness Vera Rausnitz, Prince Eddie von Holt, Oscar de la Renta, Raquel Welch, and so on, and so on. The guests partook of $12,800 worth of Beluga caviar and eighty-four bottles of the world's most expensive champagne. The whole evening is said to have cost between $50,000 and $100,000. Arm in arm with Regine, Iglesias told the group, "This lady is like a sister to me, we've known each other so long."

There was another party the night before closing night. It was a birthday dinner held *after* Julio had given two shows that evening. The celebration, which included some forty friends, lasted until 4:00 A.M., after which he went to meet his musicians who also wanted to celebrate his birthday, by the pool.

Yet none of this wee-hours activity seemed to interfere with the closing night at Resorts. Julio was musically enchanting. He was personally delightful. He asked the lighting technicians to put the lights on his legs, then said, "See how skinny. I'm a shit. When I'm told I'm a sex symbol I laugh. When I get up in the morning and I see myself in the mirror, I thank God." The audience laughed. "Wait," he continued. "Not because I believe it. I thank God because you do." This inspired a round of applause, which inspired another Julio gem: "This is the only country in the world where everyone wakes up laughing. It's great."

He sang his usual favorites—"Begin the Beguine," "As Time Goes By," "Canto a Galicia," "Cucurucucu Paloma," "When I Fall in Love," among others. When he sang "Never, Never, Never" (the English version of Tony Renis's "Grande, Grande, Grande") with his excellent vocalist Janey Clewer, he tickled her just as she was about to hit the high note. She missed the note. The audience laughed. It was all in the spirit of great fun.

The audience sang too. They sang "Happy Birthday, Julio," and a fan who shared his birthday was kissed by him three times. Said Julio, "If I get pregnant I know who did it." After this, the woman couldn't stop bubbling, telling people it was the happiest day of her life.

Julio told the audience that he was exhausted. Small wonder, after a three-month tour that had moved nonstop across the continent, and a birthday party that had taken him into the morning. But, as had happened many times earlier in the concert tour, the audience was unwilling to let go. He was so mellow. He was singing so well. Said Julio, "I come out here and I give, I give, I give." A friend of his once said of him, "He sings about love and gives it away in every performance." Nothing could have been more true that night.

By October 6, 1984, Julio Iglesias had six albums on the *Billboard* Top 200 Charts for albums and tapes. *1100 Bel Air Place* was number 6, *Julio* was number 102, *In Concert* was number 159, *From a Child to a Woman* was number 181, *Hey* was number 182, and *Momentos* was number 199. Obviously, the "language barrier" was no longer the problem it had been perceived to be.

From Atlantic City, Julio went on to the Johnny Carson show, where, among other things, Johnny asked Julio his opinion of Boy George. Julio's reply was that he loves Boy George, to which he quickly added, "In a good way, of course."

Following the Carson show was one day at Pacific Amphitheater in Costa Mesa, California, before Julio continued to Europe, Africa, and Australia.

At times Julio's energy obviously flagged, but mostly he seemed to be a storehouse of energy resources the power companies would do well to tap. His performances, both in the U.S. and abroad, were consistently well received, though the few problems that kept cropping up were noted by both fans and critics. Amplification was not always realistic, hence volume wasn't always in a comfortable range, and it was felt by many that the echo effect was overused. Also, not everyone appreciated the variety of languages in which Julio sang.

All in all, there is no question that Julio honestly tried to please *everyone*. If he's guilty of anything, he's guilty of trying so hard to please so many people in so many languages that he may spread himself too thin. Yet the point is debatable. His success in the United States has touched so many different nationalities that he has no choice but to sing in as many languages as he can manage.

The Spanish-speaking audience, quite naturally, wants to hear him in Spanish. After all, they share his roots, and it's the Spanish-speaking audience that was responsible for his initial success. Perhaps they feel he *owes* them. More important is that *he* feels he owes them, and refuses to let them down.

Other Europeans too share in his beginnings, and certainly in the momentum that carried him to superstardom. They want to hear him sing in the languages that first won them over: French, Italian, Portuguese.

It's a difficult choice. Should Julio speak to his audience in English and sing essentially in Spanish? Should he homogenize himself by speaking and singing only English? If he assembles a show that's all-English, is he supposed to change it altogether when he takes it to Europe, Africa, and the Far East? Or is it wisest to go on doing right what he's doing?

So far, leaving things as they are seems the best formula. However, Julio has never been one to settle for leaving well enough alone. He's a perfectionist, and if his presentation needs perfecting, count on him to perfect it.

Meanwhile, as he completes his demanding crossover to the United States, his long-time fans should try to be more understanding. For that matter, they should glow with pride. He's succeeded on a scale that no Latin artist has ever come close to. He's opened doors and reached heights that make him a nearly impossible act to follow.

While there have been international stars like Xavier Cugat, Edith Piaf, Yves Montand, Maurice Chevalier, José Iturbi, and Charles Aznavour, they've never reached Julio Iglesias' level of truly worldwide popularity in terms of record sales and sold-out concerts.

According to U.S. Hispanic Affairs, he "represents the first Hispanic to be wined and dined by American advertising and the American corporation on such a grandiose scale." Julio himself has said, "This is a very big country. And this is the first time a European artist has been this successful. That's never happened before, so it's an impossible dream."

Just as his longtime fans need to consider the many aspects of Julio's crossover, his newest fans need to realize that he's not about to shake off the rest of the world. The croony romantic voice, the European charm, and the Latin good looks are in his blood. His spectacular performances will always reflect that fact.

Spain misses Julio. She wants her son back. The Cubans in Miami see less of him now that he belongs to the world. Some Latin journalists have questioned this at press conferences, and have been less than satisfied with Julio's answers. Yet some U.S. journalists have berated him for the opposite reason. Every audience is pulling him in a different direction.

Pleasing all of the people all of the time is eternally impossible. But Julio Iglesias may succeed at this, too, where others before him have failed. The impossible hasn't stopped him yet.

# TWELVE

# THE
# PRODUCT OF
# SUCCESS

J ulio Iglesias comes to his fans in many forms. He can be heard on record or tape. They can opt to purchase a ticket for a performance, or buy a Julio T-shirt or other Julio souvenir in the lobby at one of his concerts. Julio is so big that he's become what anyone with such clout does become: big business.

As an artist rises from performer to star to superstar, his needs in terms of financial backing also increase. After all, one small local radio station can feature one local singer if it so chooses. But it takes an outfit like CBS International to promote a star throughout the world.

When a star is as big as Julio Iglesias, the investments made by a CBS International or a Coca-Cola Company are enormous. Even though backers may be quite wealthy, they still have to *believe* in a talent before going as far as some have with Julio.

As Sylvie Vartan, France's top female singer, has observed, "In France, you can make your own career. It's such a small country. All you have to do is a few TV shows and, if people like you,

you're a star. In America, you need an army to get yourself promoted."

Even before he broke into the U.S. market, Julio Iglesias was no kid putting on a show in the barn. And now that he *is* a U.S. hit, he's got a veritable army depending on him. He provides not only his own livelihood but that of a sizable staff. His records represent not only his own investment, but that of his collaborators, his record label, and the record stores that opt to fill window or floor space with Julio Iglesias displays. If the records don't sell, everyone involved loses money. If a concert shouldn't turn a profit, its failure will affect the technicians, musicians, vocalists, local promoters, management, and employees of whatever house he plays, and the group or organization sponsoring the performance. If the performance happens to be a charity benefit, its gross has to outstrip the initial cash outlay, or the charity is actually being deprived of money that might otherwise have gone directly into its till.

Profits are so hard to come by that many performers don't get the backing Julio enjoys until they've proved themselves beyond any reasonable doubt. It's not just backing that someone like Julio Iglesias is accorded. He's being, quite literally, banked on.

When Julio toured Spain in August 1983, his official sponsor was the Club de Vacaciones travel organization. Arrangements had to be made for the 127 musicians, technicians, bodyguards, secretaries, etc., of the troupe. It was an expensive proposition, but it paid its way. The tour's revenue was reportedly in the $2,000,000–$3,000,000 range.

When he performed in Toronto in 1984, his contract with Concert Promotions International (CPI) specified arrangements ranging from financial to culinary. But there's nothing unusual in this. It's all part of the big-money end of the music trade. That same summer in Toronto, for instance, CPI had a contract with Willie Nelson that required a "home-style sit-down meal" for performers and crew before his concert.

CPI was not the only group with a dollars-and-cents interest in Julio. The show also represented one night in Labatt's Blue Live concert series. The Labatt Brewing Company, Ltd., is not primarily in the concert business. Their product is beer. One of the ways they promote their product is by sponsoring sports events. Beginning in 1984, they ventured into the music world by sponsoring the popular concert series.

The CNE itself had an interest in offering top acts as part of its package of entertainment superlatives. Besides the performers, CNE drawing cards included The Great Canadian Breakdance Challenge; robots named Omnibot, Verbot, and Dingbot; a monster Bingo Bonanza; opportunities to enter *The Guinness Book of World Records* in categories like bubblegum blowing, milk sipping, and hula-hooping; and the gargantuan fifty-mph Double Loop Coaster roller coaster, imported from West Germany. Similarly it's the ability of the performers to make money for themselves and their associates that brings them to places like the CNE Grandstand in the first place.

Of course, the major sponsoring force behind Julio's 1984 tour was Coca-Cola. There are few sponsoring forces more major on the face of the planet. The company's sales are in the billions. Coke has been asked for by name in eighty languages. It's been calculated that if all the Coke ever downed by the human race were poured over Niagara Falls, the falls would keep going at their normal rate for nine hours.

Even so, Coca-Cola felt the need of Julio's services to bring their product to the world.

He's not their only spokesperson. James Coco, Shari Belafonte, Christie Brinkley, Tommy Lasorda, Chuck Yeager, and Duran Duran have allied themselves with the Coca-Cola camp. Even the cartoon logo from the movie *Ghostbusters* was incorporated in a promotional campaign for the soft drink. But Julio is a definite kingpin.

Announcing the three-year sponsorship arrangement between Coca-Cola and Julio Iglesias, Coke's President, Donald R. Keough, opined that, "More than likely, while people around the world are listening to Julio, they are enjoying a bottle of Coke." According to Carlton Curtis, Coca-Cola's manager of corporate communications, "Julio will create a very strong association in the minds of consumers who don't yet think of Coca-Cola as part of daily life."

In short, Coke and Julio would bring a song and a Coke to people around the world. Coke would sponsor Julio's three-year multi-continent tour. Julio would promote Coke and Diet Coke through print, radio, and TV spots. He would also join Coca-Cola, a founding sponsor of the Statue of Liberty–Ellis Island Centennial campaign, in its crusade to preserve freedom's most beloved symbol. His support would include charity concerts and fundraiser dinners. The commitment works for Julio on multiple levels, not the least of which is personal. The Statue welcomes newcomers to U.S. shores—just as the U.S. has welcomed Julio, and taken him to her heart.

Julio has been, in the words of *U.S. Hispanic Affairs*, "at the top of the charts and in the center of Madison Avenue advertising." His American conquest represents, wrote Stephen Holder in *The New York Times*, "a combined triumph of talent, marketing and timing." These three factors are a necessity before any chances can be taken, before great promise is turned into big business.

# JULIO TODAY:
# MUSIC FOR
# THE WORLD

*W*hen a star like Julio Iglesias records a duet with a star like Diana Ross or Willie Nelson, all parties stand to gain in the event of success. But in the event of failure, the trouble is multiplied, even affecting the armies who depend on each of the participating stars.

Yet in the case of Julio Iglesias, the risks taken were justified. The Iglesias–Nelson duet single "To All the Girls I've Loved Before" placed number one on the Country Charts, number five on the Pop Charts, and won the Country Music Award for Vocal Duo of the Year. In the U.S. it sold over a million copies, and it went gold and platinum in Canada.

Likewise, the Iglesias–Ross duet single "All of You" hit two charts, both *Billboard*'s Pop Charts and Adult Contemporary. Enthused *Billboard*, "It's time for the tender emotions as suave European balladry meets silken American soul." The single led to the "All of You" video starring Julio Iglesias and Diana Ross, directed by Bob Giraldi, one of the hottest forces in video today. Giraldi's credits include Michael Jackson's much talked about

"Beat It," Jermaine Jackson's "Dynamite" (shot in New Jersey's Essex County Jail), and work with Paul McCartney and Lionel Richie.

The album *1100 Bel Air Place*, which includes both duets, entered the charts at number 41 on the first week of release, zoomed up to number 10 by the second week, and continued to climb. Understandably, it was a favorite on the U.S. Latin charts as well. The album reached number 1 in Denmark, number 3 in Australia, number 4 in Canada, number 6 in the Netherlands, number 2 in Spain, number 9 in West Germany, number 18 in Italy, number 37 in Britain and rising.

Meanwhile, Julio's "Moonlight Lady," written by Albert Hammond and Carole Bayer Sager—Julio's first solo single for the U.S. market—has hit the charts and inspired a video. Julio filmed this in New York, at two different locations, just prior to commencing his European '84 tour. One location was the Convent of the Sacred Heart on Manhattan's Upper East Side. Formerly a mansion, it lent itself beautifully to the lush ballroom atmosphere required to create the right mood. The second location was the U.S.S. *Empire*, docked in the Bronx. Directed by Steve Horn, produced by Linda Horn, the video stars Julio—of course—and Ford model Eva Johansson as the "Moonlight Lady" of the song.

A second Iglesias-Nelson duet single, "As Time Goes By," was recorded, pressed, and shipped. But CBS pulled all commercial copies when it was decided that the timing, that all-important component of success, was not quite right.

On television, a program for the whole Hispanic world was broadcast on Día de la Hispanidad, October 12, 1984. It starred the two foremost entertainers of the Hispanic world, Julio Iglesias and Plácido Domingo. Plácido Domingo flew from New York to tape his portion of the show in Santo Domingo, in a Roman amphitheater. Julio flew from Berlin to Seville, arriving at 3:45 in the morning. To bring this about, the authorities of the Berlin airport lifted their restriction forbidding aircraft to take off after 11:00 P.M.

Julio and his entourage, which included Italian singer-composer-producer Tony Renis and Spanish singer-composer-producer Ramón Arcusa, were sped from Seville to Huelva, to the monastery of La Rabida, where the filming was to take place. After taping and reviewing the show, Julio was dissatisfied with one of the songs. To the surprise of the TV crew and audience, he suggested taking it from the top, redoing the entire show. He's often said that pride is a defect in human relationships, but in one's profession, it's a virtue. Julio, a perfectionist, takes pride in his work, and hates to settle for anything short of the best.

Future plans include a recording of English lyrics to "Tara's Theme" from *Gone With the Wind*; perfecting his English (which Julio jokes is already perfect for him, but not yet to American ears); more records, more television, more videos, more tours. But not, so far, any more movies, though offers keep pouring in.

Julio continues to collect gold and platinum discs throughout the world. Though gold and platinum discs represent different sales depending on the country, for instance—

USA: gold single 1,000,000; gold album 500,000
   platinum single 2,000,000; platinum album 1,000,000
Canada: gold single 50,000; gold album 50,000
   platinum single 100,000; platinum album 100,000
Spain: gold single 100,000; gold album 50,000
   platinum single 150,000; platinum album 100,000
Japan: no official gold/platinum system in the Japanese recording industry

—there is no disputing the overall volume of Julio's worldwide sales.

Some critics say that the success of Julio Iglesias has been nothing more than a marketing blitz, that it is pure fabrication. Many have believed this for years. But the history of the music business is glutted with people who invested huge bankrolls in one sweeping marketing blitz or another, reaping nothing but bankruptcy as the reward. This is not the case with Julio, who has brought

profits to almost everyone associated with him. Nor can Julio's track record be pure fabrication in light of the *Guinness Book of World Records* Diamond Disc for 100,000,000 albums sold.

There is no question that, from time to time, record companies, public relations firms, and even people directly working with an artist have paid individuals to go to concerts and tapings of programs to demonstrate zealous admiration. But Julio has been packing houses for years, with people traveling great distances and waiting hour upon hour to buy tickets to his shows. He's one man who definitely doesn't need to pay people to be his fans.

He's also someone who may soon have competition.

Julio Iglesias may be a legend, but he's no myth. He is a giant among giants in a highly competitive industry. And these giants, though not all are well known in the U.S., are big successes nonetheless.

Music's superstars of Latin America include Camilo Sesto (who played the highly praised lead in the Spanish version of *Jesus Christ Superstar* in Madrid in 1975 and to date has sold over 10,000,000 records of his various titles worldwide); Miguel Ríos (who gained recognition in the U.S. during the '70s with his version of the last movement from Beethoven's Ninth Symphony, "Song of Joy," and whose 1982 double album *Rock and Ríos* sold over 400,000 copies); Joan Manuel Serrat; Luis Eduardo Aute; Juan Pardo; Raphael; and the list goes on.

In Mexico, there's José José, who has successfully played the U.S., for instance in Atlantic City. Venezuela's José Luis Rodríquez, "El Puma," this year performed for First Lady Nancy Reagan at the annual Congressional Club Luncheon. José Luis not only sings, he also happens to be one of the most sought-after actors in Latin soap operas.

In Brazil, Julio's top competition is "O Rei" (The King) Roberto Carlos, who averages a minimum of 2,000,000 in sales a year in Brazil alone. Together with co-writer Erasmo Carlos, Roberto has composed some of the most beautiful love ballads of all time. Another Brazilian, Morris Albert, gave us the standard "Feelings" and won a cover fight with Andy Williams, sold over 2,000,000 singles in the U.S. before even showing his face to the American public. "Feelings" has become one of the most re-recorded songs in music history.

Perhaps as Julio Iglesias breaks through the language barrier that has so long prevented Latin America's top stars from major U.S. success, we'll be hearing more from these talents. According to Roberto Carlos, "You have to take your hat off to Julio. He has done an incredible job. There is no question that he has opened the doors for other foreign acts to follow."

In October 1984, Julio Iglesias had six albums on *Billboard*'s Top 200 charts, one of the largest totals in history for a male singer. Barry Manilow had five in May 1977. John Denver had six in December 1975. There were seven Elvis Presley albums on the charts simultaneously in October 1977, and six John Lennon albums on the charts in February 1981, but in each case, the surge of interest in the performers came on the heels of their untimely and tragic death.

Realistically speaking, in terms of total multilanguage worldwide numbers, Julio Iglesias outsells everybody. In terms of music, he's not in competition with people who don't sing anything remotely similar to his repertoire. His is—and this indisputably contributes to his U.S. success—filling a void.

He sings in the tradition of Frank Sinatra, Tony Bennett, Vic Damone, Nat King Cole, and Johnny Mathis. "His lushly crooning romantic style" (Brian Chin, *New York Post*) strikes emotional gold (and platinum). "He can stroke a melody with legato tenderness or let a note curl and break like a wave on the beach" (*Newsweek*).

On stage, he projects romance across the footlights and out to the farthest upper-mezzanine seat. His charm and sex appeal "would probably be enough to make even the croakings of Kermit the Frog sound like satin" (*Time* Magazine).

In February, Julio was chosen by *Good Housekeeping* as one of "The 50 Most Eligible Bachelors," putting him in the illustrious company of Eddie Murphy, Lee Iacocca, and Michael Jackson.

In March, it was reported that Julio would have to cut back on

# CONQUERING AMERICA

his U
of $
r

9t
mu
America
artists Ba
Los Herman
World) met at
geles—the same s
done. The song, "C
sing") is in Spanish wit

Among the impressive r
voices for "Cantaré, Cantará
Roberto Carlos, Vicente Fernán
guez, José José, Emmanuel, Pedro
Jurado, Lisette, Celia Cruz, Simone,
Ramón Arcusa, Basilio, Palito Ortega,
Schifrin. Among the actors lending their
moment were Ricardo Montalban, Mario (Ca
and Cheech Marin (of Cheech and Chong). Plácid
Menudo, though unable to attend due to previous
mitments, offered to add their voices in post-producti

He continues to be called "The Spanish Sinatra." But
one hears an occasional, "Hey, listen, that's 'Strangers in
Night,' sung by the American Julio Iglesias.'"

The Bettmann Archive

Peter C. Borsari

*Diana Ross and Julio from the cover of their single "All Of You" (opposite page). Julio visiting Johnny Carson on the "Tonight Show" (top). Julio charming Ursula Andress and Joan Collins (above).*

Ebet Roberts

Ron Galella

Peter C. Borsari

*Joining the Beach Boys in song during the July 4th celebrations in Washington D.C. From left to right, Bruce Jonston, Brian Wilson, Carl Wilson, Al Jardine and Mike Love (top). Julio gallantly greets debutante socialite, Cornelia Guest (middle). The Beach Boys gave Julio an autographed surfboard after the recording of "The Air That I Breathe" (left).*

Ebet Roberts

*Julio is enthralled by festivities and audience at the Washington Monument (left). Diana Ross joined Julio on stage at Radio City Music Hall for a quick peck on the cheek before they debuted their "All Of You" video for the audience (middle). With La Toya Jackson and Mike Love on stage in Washington, D.C. (bottom).*

Gary Gershoff/Retna Ltd.

Ebet Roberts

*M*rs. Frank Sinatra poses with Julio during the World Mercy Fund Benefit (left). New York's Mayor Edward Koch and Diana Ross congratulate Julio backstage at Radio City (bottom).

Ron Galella

Gary Gershoff/Retna Ltd.

*M*rs. Frank Sinatra poses with Julio during the World Mercy Fund Benefit (left). New York's Mayor Edward Koch and Diana Ross congratulate Julio backstage at Radio City (bottom).

Ron Galella

Gary Gershoff/Retna Ltd.

*J*ulio is enthralled by festivities and audience at the Washington Monument (left). Diana Ross joined Julio on stage at Radio City Music Hall for a quick peck on the cheek before they debuted their "All Of You" video for the audience (middle). With La Toya Jackson and Mike Love on stage in Washington, D.C. (bottom).

Ebet Roberts

Gary Gershoff/Retna Ltd.

Ebet Roberts

Ebet Roberts

Ron Galella

Peter C. Borsari

Joining the Beach Boys in song during the July 4th celebrations in Washington D.C. From left to right, Bruce Jonston, Brian Wilson, Carl Wilson, Al Jardine and Mike Love (top). Julio gallantly greets debutante socialite, Cornelia Guest (middle). The Beach Boys gave Julio an auto-graphed surfboard after the recording of "The Air That I Breathe" (left).

The Bettmann Archive

Peter C. Borsari

*D*iana Ross and Julio from the cover of
their single "All Of You" (opposite page).
Julio visiting Johnny Carson on the "Tonight
Show" (top). Julio charming Ursula Andress
and Joan Collins (above).

# CONQUERING AMERICA

his U.S. tour plans, which had brought him in the neighborhood of $175,000 a night. The worldwide demand for Julio had reached new heights, and it was simply no longer possible for him to be everywhere at once. Beside dates in England, Japan, Scandinavia, and Australia, he had albums to finish.

Between March and April, Julio was in Nassau, putting the finishing touches of his long-awaited Spanish album. He also spent a few days in Rio de Janeiro, where he began work on his Portuguese album.

Yet as staggeringly busy as Julio was, he took time on April 9th to join forces with other members of the Spanish music community in the heroic battle against sickness and hunger in Latin America and Africa. Inspired by the British and American rock artists Band Aid and USA for Africa's "We Are The World," Los Hermanos Del Tercer Mundo (The Brothers Of The Third World) met at the A&M Records recording studio in Los Angeles—the same studio where "We Are The World" had been done. The song, "Cantaré, Cantarás" ("I will sing, You will sing") is in Spanish with a chorus in English and Portuguese.

Among the impressive roster of musical talents blending their voices for "Cantaré, Cantarás"—49 in all—were Julio Iglesias, Roberto Carlos, Vicente Fernández, José Luis (El Puma) Rodríguez, José José, Emmanuel, Pedro Vargas, José Feliciano, Rocio Jurado, Lisette, Celia Cruz, Simone, Gal Costa, Sergio Mendez, Ramón Arcusa, Basilio, Palito Ortega, Vickki Carr, and Lalo Schifrin. Among the actors lending their presence to the great moment were Ricardo Montalban, Mario (Cantinflas) Moreno, and Cheech Marin (of Cheech and Chong). Plácido Domingo and Menudo, though unable to attend due to previous prior commitments, offered to add their voices in post-production.

He continues to be called "The Spanish Sinatra." But already one hears an occasional, "Hey, listen, that's 'Strangers in the Night,' sung by the American Julio Iglesias.'"

singles in the U.S. before even showing his face to the American public. "Feelings" has become one of the most re-recorded songs in music history.

Perhaps as Julio Iglesias breaks through the language barrier that has so long prevented Latin America's top stars from major U.S. success, we'll be hearing more from these talents. According to Roberto Carlos, "You have to take your hat off to Julio. He has done an incredible job. There is no question that he has opened the doors for other foreign acts to follow."

In October 1984, Julio Iglesias had six albums on *Billboard*'s Top 200 charts, one of the largest totals in history for a male singer. Barry Manilow had five in May 1977. John Denver had six in December 1975. There were seven Elvis Presley albums on the charts simultaneously in October 1977, and six John Lennon albums on the charts in February 1981, but in each case, the surge of interest in the performers came on the heels of their untimely and tragic death.

Realistically speaking, in terms of total multilanguage world-wide numbers, Julio Iglesias outsells everybody. In terms of music, he's not in competition with people who don't sing anything remotely similar to his repertoire. His is—and this indisputably contributes to his U.S. success—filling a void.

He sings in the tradition of Frank Sinatra, Tony Bennett, Vic Damone, Nat King Cole, and Johnny Mathis. "His lushly crooning romantic style" (Brian Chin, *New York Post*) strikes emotional gold (and platinum). "He can stroke a melody with legato tenderness or let a note curl and break like a wave on the beach" (*Newsweek*).

On stage, he projects romance across the footlights and out to the farthest upper-mezzanine seat. His charm and sex appeal "would probably be enough to make even the croakings of Kermit the Frog sound like satin" (*Time* Magazine).

In February, Julio was chosen by *Good Housekeeping* as one of "The 50 Most Eligible Bachelors," putting him in the illustrious company of Eddie Murphy, Lee Iacocca, and Michael Jackson.

In March, it was reported that Julio would have to cut back on profits to almost everyone associated with him. Nor can Julio's track record be pure fabrication in light of the *Guinness Book of World Records* Diamond Disc for 100,000,000 albums sold.

There is no question that, from time to time, record companies, public relations firms, and even people directly working with an artist have paid individuals to go to concerts and tapings of programs to demonstrate zealous admiration. But Julio has been packing houses for years, with people traveling great distances and waiting hour upon hour to buy tickets to his shows. He's one man who definitely doesn't need to pay people to be his fans.

He's also someone who may soon have competition.

Julio Iglesias may be a legend, but he's no myth. He is a giant among giants in a highly competitive industry. And these giants, though not all are well known in the U.S., are big successes nonetheless.

Music's superstars of Latin America include Camilo Sesto (who played the highly praised lead in the Spanish version of *Jesus Christ Superstar* in Madrid in 1975 and to date has sold over 10,000,000 records of his various titles worldwide); Miguel Ríos (who gained recognition in the U.S. during the '70s with his version of the last movement from Beethoven's Ninth Symphony, "Song of Joy," and whose 1982 double album *Rock and Ríos* sold over 400,000 copies); Joan Manuel Serrat; Luis Eduardo Aute; Juan Pardo; Raphael; and the list goes on.

In Mexico, there's José José, who has successfully played the U.S., for instance in Atlantic City. Venezuela's José Luis Rodríquez, "El Puma," this year performed for First Lady Nancy Reagan at the annual Congressional Club Luncheon. José Luis not only sings, he also happens to be one of the most sought-after actors in Latin soap operas.

In Brazil, Julio's top competition is "O Rei" (The King) Roberto Carlos, who averages a minimum of 2,000,000 in sales a year in Brazil alone. Together with co-writer Erasmo Carlos, Roberto has composed some of the most beautiful love ballads of all time. Another Brazilian, Morris Albert, gave us the standard "Feelings" and won a cover fight with Andy Williams, sold over 2,000,000

Elizabeth Garcia

*A*ll smiles at Regine's party honoring Julio (left). What could Joan Collins have been saying to Julio? (above) Just a warm smile for his fans (bottom).

Peter C. Borsari

H. Gallo/Shooting Star

*Ron Galella*

*C*harles Aznavour was on hand to celebrate Julio's 40th Birthday (left). With Brooke Shields after his opening in Los Angeles (below).

*Jim Asher/Celebrity Photo*

AP/Wide World Photos

Fotos International/Pictorial Parade, Inc.

*Premiering "To All the Girls I've Loved Before" with Willie Nelson at the Country Music Awards in Nashville (above). The "seductive look"...(left).*

# FOURTEEN

# JULIO
# TODAY:
# THE MAN

Julio Iglesias the boy was a postwar baby of the first modern-weapons war in the history of the world. As a young man, Julio was a soccer star with a promising future as a "jock," but this future was cut short by a horrendous auto accident.

Today, Julio Iglesias the man is a superstar jet-setter, a man so closely meshed with his music, his market, and his show that he's often seen as the sum total of these three components.

Yet, on or off the treadmill of superstardom, Julio remains, quite simply, a man.

He is superstitious. He knocks on wood or touches his boot before performing, flying, or undertaking any make-him-or-break-him endeavor. He's said to leave the table when salt is spilled, or to react to bad news by removing the clothes he's wearing, however expensive, and destroying them.

He's been called "the most caring, affectionate person I have known in my life" by *Cosmpolitan Español*'s Cristina Saralegui, who considers few families as physically demonstrative in their affections as the Iglesias family. Julio's outgoingness in this respect has startled some U.S. eyes, with *Newsweek* describing him on stage as looking like he was "cursed with Doctor Strangelove's runaway hand."

Julio has told reporters that his three grand passions in life are "my children, the sun, and women."

Much has been written on the subject of Julio and women, some of it no doubt true, some of it apparently inflated. A few years ago, Julio was photographed allegedly enjoying a hush–hush tryst with British beauty queen Carolyn Seaward. A hot romance was rumored. The rumor was followed by a statement to the papers from Miss Seaward, pointing out that the picture was misleading, as she had been just one member of a dinner party attended by Julio.

Through the years, Julio's name has been linked romantically with a long list of foreign beauties and, depending on what papers you read, Diana Ross and Brooke Shields. Virginia Sipl, of Venezuela, seemed to rank high on the list for years. Others seen on the list have included Vaitiaré, a Tahitian; Italian actress Sidney Rome; and 1977 Miss World, Marie Stavins of Sweden (who rescues James Bond in a minisub in the Roger Moore 007 epic *A View to Kill*).

As Isabel Preysler, his former wife (now Marquesa de Griñón), has told the press, "Julio likes women more than is normal, but I don't believe everything that is printed."

Speaking of love, Julio has said that he has to be in love continually to feel alive, but that to be in love doesn't necessarily imply great love. For now, "I have a thousand women, but not The One, not The Woman." Considering his demanding schedule, the sort of great love that leads to marriage could constitute a monumental inconvenience for Julio at the moment.

Julio presently owns several houses around the world but feels, "I have houses, not homes." His real home seems to be a Mystere-Falcon 20, which jets him to his endless commitments on six continents. After sixteen years of this kind of life, he's used to it, though he has never developed a love for flying.

He's close to his family, particularly to his children, his brother, and his parents. Julio's mother, Rosario ("Charo") de la Cueva, spends much of her time at his Miami home, or at the Miami home of Julio's brother Carlos. Charo is an outgoing hostess, known for her sense of humor and her devotion to both her sons. Recently she shared Julio's favorite recipes with readers of *Vanidades* magazine, so his fans would know what to prepare in case he dropped by. The recipes included *tortilla española* (a Spanish omelette made with eggs and fried potatoes), *paella* (made with shrimp, clams, mussels, chicken, pork, saffron, and rice), and *gazpacho* (a cold soup made with tomatoes, green peppers, onions, and cucumbers). Julio is decidedly partial to seafood, and to Spanish and Latin American cuisine.

Julio's father, Dr. Julio Iglesias-Puga, is a respected gynecologist, semi-retired now, who often accompanies his son on tour.

Julio's brother, Dr. Carlos Iglesias, is an indispensable person in Julio's life. Carlos, a physician for years, gave up his practice in order to handle Julio's business affairs. Like Julio, he lives in Miami. Carlos is two years younger—and, some say, is handsomer—than Julio. Economists and financial advisors work closely with him to judge how best to invest Julio's earnings. Moreover, Carlos "runs interference" for Julio, fielding all the demands and requests that come his way. These range from the reasonable to the ridiculous, and it falls to Carlos to pass the appropriate ones on to Julio.

One of Carlos's other chief responsibilities is saying no. He is, in effect, the official "heavy" of the organization, and in that capacity has been criticized on occasion by the press. In an article in the Spanish tabloid *Interviu*, an ex-majordomo claimed that certain articles would disappear from Julio's home for no reason and then reappear in the home of Carlos. According to the ex-majordomo, the dubious explanation given by Carlos was that Julio had gotten tired of these things.

When Dr. Iglesias, Sr., heard about the story, he hastened to his son's defense. He said that a person who would tell such a story obviously has no scruples, and that the reason the man was an *ex*-majordomo was because he'd taken advantage of the Iglesias family in the past.

According to Dr. Iglesias, Sr., people who speak badly of his sons don't know his sons. He suggests that rather than heeding the lies of disgruntled ex-employees, people should question the people working now for Julio and Carlos. They would discover that both Julio and Carlos consistently exhibit warm, wonderful qualities.

Julio has been a resident of the Miami area since 1978. His house is located on the ultra-exclusive private island of Indian Creek. Carlos has a home on the same island, not far away. When first deciding to live in Florida, Julio had his eye on Fort Lauderdale. But when he saw the property on Indian Creek—with beach and sun, both so appealing to Julio—he was enchanted.

Indian Creek, a magicial kingdom under the golden sun, boasts million-dollar mansions, a golf course shaded by thousand-year-old trees, and breathtaking views of Biscayne Bay. Access to the island, whether by land or by sea, is impossible without previous consent of an island resident. The bridge connecting it to Miami Beach is overseen by a control booth manned twenty-four hours a day. Special security police detain all guests until clearance is obtained from the island resident being visited. There are boats patrolling the bay. In addition, Julio has security guards in his private employ.

Julio's home, a $3 to 5 million, seven-bedroom mansion, is one of the more spectacular on Indian Creek. Inside are vast space, splendid, casual furnishings, Spanish artwork, stereo and recording equipment, and a lifetime's collection of plaques, trophies, and awards. The mansion features three swimming pools: one is for Julio's private use; a second, located in the interior patio, is a favorite eating and lounging spot; and a third is located beside the yacht-filled bay. One of Julio's yachts, *Chaveli*, is named after his daughter. The other yacht, *La Flaca* (Skinny Lady), is said to be named for Virginia Sipl. Julio has two boats so that, if he is using one, the other can be at the disposal of friends or guests.

Though he is surrounded by the trappings of elegant leisure, Julio feels the pressure of his schedule, and thus lives like a man in a hurry. His press manager, Fernán Martínez, tells of the time Julio decided the water in his pool was too warm. Fernán offered to lower the temperature control. Julio felt this would take too much time, and instead had tons of ice dumped into the pool. On another occasion, when the grounds were being landscaped, Julio had 300 fully grown palm trees planted because he didn't feel he had time to wait for trees to grow.

When a reporter asked Julio about his home a few years ago, Julio answered, with something akin to remorse, "When I was finishing the house, I was engrossed in the work and very happy. But once the house was redone I suddenly got very depressed. . . . Everything had been finished."

Julio Iglesias is a man who thrives on beginning new challenges. He's not one to relish endings.

Since his divorce from Isabel, Julio sees his three children less than he would like but as much as is humanly possible.

Earlier this year, Julio, accompanied by his father, took time out from his hectic schedule to fly to Madrid for his son Enrique's first communion. There was a choir of four girls who sang during the ceremony. At the end of the sacrament, they asked Julio for his autograph. He very graciously complied, but told them that they were the artists of the day. He was only the father.

Isabel Preysler, today the wife of the Marques of Griñón (whom she had been dating when Julio first saw her), visited Julio this year at his Indian Creek home. She came with her four children. (She has another daughter, Tamara, from her second marriage.) Chaveli, Enrique, and Julio José were thrilled to see their father again.

The reason for the visit to Indian Creek was to drop off Chaveli, Enrique, and Julio José to spend part of their holidays with their father, and also to make arrangements for their futures. Chaveli will be attending private school in London, one well known among children of royal blood and heirs to great fortunes. The name of the school will be withheld from the press for reasons of security.

Julio is proud of Chaveli, a beautiful girl, and appreciates the way Isabel has brought her up. Three years away from college, she's at a vulnerable and impressionable age that gives Julio some concern. He's expressed the hope that she will trust him and tell him everything.

Julio's two sons, Enrique and Julio José, will remain at Indian Creek. There they will study in the school attended by their cousins, the children of Carlos Iglesias. Julio José, sociable and extroverted, would like to become a soccer player. Enrique, less outgoing than his brother, prefers electronic games and race cars.

Both Julio and Isabel want all three of their children to perfect their English, a language they believe is imperative in today's world.

Doña Charo, Julio's mother, is delighted that her grandsons will be in Miami. Together with Carlos' children, they fill her with grandmotherly pride. Said Julio to the press, "I hope that now, with my children, I will find the home I lost."

Besides the Miami property, Julio owns a ranch in Argentina and is having a home completed in the Bahamas. There are rumors that he might be acquiring a *pazo gallego* (Galician palace) in Galicia, Spain, and a mansion in Los Angeles. Always, he is adamant that his children should have the best rooms. Wherever they are living at a given moment, he likes the rooms to be ready for their arrival, as though they were living there all the time. He wants them to know that his houses are their homes.

Julio works hard at his craft, investing long, arduous hours in recording, composing, and performing. Between tours, he records between five and ten albums a year in different languages. Though his appearances are infrequent in markets like Argentina, Mexico, and Spain—markets that once commanded so much of his time—he continues to be active all over the world. Some would call him a glutton for punishment, but Julio maintains that nothing stimulates him more than his work.

When possible, he exercises to keep up his stamina. Speaking of one tour, he explained, "You're either in the best of shape when you start out, or you'll never make it through a tour like this." He pushes himself beyond reasonable endurance, even admitting that the taxing effort may take its toll. "Because I'm not a young artist, I'm going to lose maybe four, five, six, ten years of my life."

By all accounts, Julio Iglesias today is where he fought most of his life to be. "He's the biggest seller on the CBS Records Group roster—bigger than Barbra Streisand, Paul McCartney, or Michael Jackson" (*Esquire*, February 1984). How many of his albums have sold? "Millions? Trillions? Zillions? Who knows? Not even Julio" (*Miami News*, September 1982).

Julio Iglesias is Don Quijote, master of his quest. No longer must he dream the impossible dream. The dream is possible. He proved it. He can quit whenever he wants to. There may be nothing left to prove.

It's tempting to speculate on what Julio will do next. More records, videos, and concert tours, surely. A movie? His movie career was brief and unrewarding, so he says no to future movies. Another marriage? Julio says he'll remarry when Johnny Carson does—to which Johnny replies that, in that case, he's going to be lonely.

Not long ago it was reported that Julio Iglesias had written his own epitaph: "I stopped dreaming when I could buy my dreams."

Maybe. But his fans don't believe it for a minute. To them, he's still a lover who makes love to the world, a dreamer who makes dreams happen.

He's still Don Quijote.

He's still Don Juan.

# RAFAEL
# REVERT

R afael Revert is responsible for programming 136 radio stations in Spain. He has known Julio Iglesias since the very beginning of his career. The following interview, exclusive for this book, took place in July 1984.

Q: Which are the top-ranking solo artists in Spain?

RR: Actually, it hasn't varied much in recent years. It is still Julio Iglesias, Joan Manuel Serrat, Camilo Sesto, Eduardo Aute, Juan Pardo, José Luis Perales, and Bertin Osborne.

Q: What do you think of the Julio Iglesias phenomenon?

RR: I think it's great. Every time that there is a Spaniard out there who is successful, it means that another one can follow. It is phenomenal and I'm thrilled for him. I believe the whole country is thrilled for him, particularly since it's the result of years of hard work, careful planning, thinking things out, and then doing them right. It's quite an accomplishment.

Q: Has "To All the Girls I've Loved Before" been a hit in Spain?

RR: Right now it's number three on the charts. Yes, it has been a hit. Actually, there are two or three songs which are vying for the number-one position at this time. We're just waiting to see if it will make it to number one.

Q: How about "All of You"?

RR: It was released last week and shows great promise.

Q: What type of dance music, if any, is popular in Spain?

RR: Disco music. Disco music as it is recorded in Europe. Italy has a great deal of influence on our dance music. Germany has some too. Disco music is big in general, especially those technopop groups. However, *salsa* has never made it here. You'd think it would, but it never has taken off.

Q: What was Julio like at the beginning of his career?

RR: He was stupendous. He would come, often, to the radio station. I remember he would come often to "El Gran Musical" [a weekly radio broadcast, considered to be the most important in Spain, done live before an audience. "El Gran Musical" offers guest artists the chance to break a new release or sing a song that's already made it onto the charts]. He was always concerned about his career. I remember that he was just beginning and he came to me with his first single, and asked, "Rafael, what do you think this will sell?" I answered, "Fifteen to twenty thousand." It was always his biggest worry.

Q: Did you ever think he would make it so big?

RR: No, not at first. Not until I saw him perform at the Fiesta Palace in Mexico City. I believe it was his third or fourth trip there. That's when I fully understood his potential. Of course, I never imagined he'd be number one all over the world. But one could feel that he would go far. He was the only one who absolutely knew he could do it. Perhaps his manager, Alfredo Fraile, had a strong hunch too. No one else did, not that I know of.

Q: Would you have any anecdotes about him?

RR: Sure. He had a habit—I'm sure he's broken it long since—but when he first started in the business, he used to do this and I found it really amusing.

He'd come over and visit us at the radio station and afterwards we'd go to this cafe-bar that was across the street. Whenever he would enter this place, his main objective, his preoccupation, was to be recognized. So he'd go up to people and say, "Listen, madam, listen, mister, do you know who I am?"

More often than not, the person would answer, "No. I have no idea who you are."

He'd answer, "What do you mean you don't know who I am. I'm Julio Iglesias."

This must have made quite an impression. From one person he'd go on to another, and another. The funny thing is that he promoted himself very effectively this way. He'd win over the customers, one by one.

His need to be famous was really fundamental to him. He always wanted to be famous.

Q: Now he's famous. What does Spain feel about the success he's attained?

RR: There's a large majority enjoying it. They're proud because he's a Spaniard. The people are thrilled and happy. The Spanish music industry is also very pleased that he's made it. But, of course, there are always some who don't like him. It's their opinion. Maybe it's a little envy, too. When someone's as visible as he is all over the world, it's a given that such a feeling is bound to exist.

Q: What is your opinion of him?

RR: He's sharp, clever. He may be the brightest guy I know when it comes to songs, to the music business. He's a hard worker. He's been able to create a style that is totally personal. He hasn't copied it from anyone. It's him. This in itself is very difficult. As an artist, there isn't anyone who comes close.

In the whole world, I don't believe that there's an artist so preoccupied with his work that he studies everything. Iglesias knows and understands every aspect of his field. He's involved in everything. I don't believe there is anyone like him, who's sacrificed so much. If that person exists, I've never met him . . . or her.

Q: What is Julio Iglesias like on a social level?

RR: He's at the highest social level imaginable. He is a man who is seen elbowing with royalty and heads of state.

Q: With the worldwide simultaneous release of *1100 Bel Air Place* that has been scheduled, do you think he'll be able to have the

album in the number-one slot simultaneously around the world?
RR: Besides the great work he's done on the album, you must keep in mind that CBS also does great work. They're a very strong combination. I believe he has a 99 percent chance of doing it.
Q: What's the secret of his success?
RR: To my mind, it's his work. Perseverance in his work. A great desire to succeed. Julio had such a great desire to be what he is that he had to get it. I have always said that in life you are what you propose to be, what you set out to be. If you propose to do something with all your will, with all your strength, setting that goal above everything else, you'll make it. His goal was to be number one all over the world.

He used to joke with me and say that he'd succeed the way Elvis Presley did. He knew how much I admired Presley and the Rolling Stones. So that was his refrain to me: "I'll be as famous as Elvis Presley and the Rolling Stones." I'd laugh. But he knew. He has fought hard for it. The secret to his success has been his work. That desire to be above all others without resting or taking time out for himself, without his family, without his friends. He has fought all his life for this. Very few people would fight as hard. That's how he reached his goal.
Q: Would you like to say something to Julio?
RR: What can I say? He knows that we love him here. That we get annoyed with him every now and then when when we don't see him in Spain as much as we'd like. But later we reconcile. Always, we support him.

# GERHARD
# HALTERMANN

Gerhard Haltermann, presently an owner of Discos Victoria, was Director of Promotion when Julio Iglesias first came to Discos Columbia. They worked together for eleven years. This interview, recalling those years, took place in Madrid in July 1984.

Q: What was Julio Iglesias like when you knew him?

GH: He knows how to win people over. Especially females. He always has the right word, and delivers it at the right moment. He's a charmer. I have seen him with an elderly woman in the lobby of a hotel in Germany. At the perfect moment, he leaned down and gave her a kiss and hug. Naturally, that woman will hardly refer to him as unfeeling.

Julio knows how to do it real well. He's very careful about his image.

Q: Can you tell me a little about his work?

GH: He thoroughly enjoys performing on stage. Julio is the kind of person who, I don't know, he absolutely thrives on audience applause.

Q: How does he manage to be number one in so many markets?
GH: Charisma. His productions are good. They never go out of style. His public is one that's obviously over thirty. He represents the image of a Latin lover well. He has enjoyed representing that role and he does it to perfection.

Q: Have you ever witnessed any of Julio's superstitions?
GH: It has nothing to do with superstition, but I know he doesn't like to fly. I remember once when we were flying to Brussels. This was after there had been an unfortunate incident with the controllers, where an aircraft of Iberia and a Spantax charter carrier collided. This was on our minds as we flew, but we were ourselves quite calm. It was around two in the afternoon. Our seat belts were fastened. We were eating. All of a sudden, the plane descended, plunged, very rapidly. Almost as if it had hit an air pocket. Trays went flying every which way. The flight attendants had fallen and were rolling down the aisles. Later we found out what had happened. The pilot came on over the intercom, apologizing and explaining that he had seen an aircraft that hadn't appeared on the radar screen. When he saw the thing, it was coming right at us. If he hadn't done all that maneuvering, we may have collided.

Julio may be superstitious about flying. He surely doesn't enjoy it. But he is very professional and does it anyhow, because he knows it's part of his work.

Q: What's he like to work with?
GH: He's a perfectionist and likes things done correctly. In other words, if at a given moment things have not been done as he has requested, he gets very annoyed and ill-tempered, but with good reason. But the moment things are ready and running on schedule, smoothly, there's never any problem.

Also, he dislikes being photographed on the left side, and I recall once when we were taping a program in Germany, he asked me to advise the photographer accordingly. His right side is his better profile.

Q: Where was his first album recorded?
GH: Part of it was recorded in Madrid, but later it was completed at the Decca Studios in London.

Q: What about his first hit, "La Vida Sigue Igual"?

GH: Actually, Los Gritos made a hit of it before Julio did. This was the group that performed the song with him at the Benidorm Festival in 1968. At that time, each song at the festival had to be performed twice. "La Vida Sigue Igual" was done once by Julio, and another time by this group. They were a known band, and back then were more experienced than Julio, so they recorded the song, and it did extremely well. This was followed by Julio's success with the song.

Q: And then Julio went on to the Eurovision Festival in March 1970.

GH: He represented Spain at Eurovision in March 1970, from the seventeenth to the twenty-second. It was held at the Congress-Centrum in Amsterdam. Julio sang the song "Gwendolyne," composed by him and dedicated to the girl he'd met and loved while studying in the United Kingdom. Julio finished fourth at Eurovision. The winner was an Irish girl named Dana. Her song was "All Kinds of Everything."

Q: Have other Spanish artists done well at Eurovision?

GH: Both Massiel and Raphael had great luck there, Massiel with "La, La, La" and Raphael with "Yo Soy Aquel."

Q: Do you have anything you'd like to say to Julio Iglesias?

GH: I wish him continued success. I have always admired the man. As an artist, he gives himself entirely to his public, and that is what has made him so successful.

# ENRIQUE GAREA

*E*nrique Garea was A&R Manager, later General Manager, of Discos Columbia when Julio Iglesias was associated with the label. Garea, who remains General Manager of Discos Columbia, gave this interview in Madrid in July 1984.

Q: What is Julio like as a friend?

EG: Julio is a good friend, and good to his friends. He has never forgotten those who have helped him. He has helped many in times of need, economically or in other ways. He is still close to many that were with him from the beginning—for instance, look at his musical director, Rafael Ferro, who has shared the stage with him all these years. He is always with him. All those day-to-day problems, they resolve them, and they work extremely well together.

When Julio first bought his home in Miami, I was there in Miami on a business trip. I called to say hello. He went to pick me up in his Rolls. And he said, "I have another one, you know." To this I responded, "Why didn't you bring them both? How else will people know you have two of them, if one isn't trailing right behind the other?"

He took me to this beautiful restaurant for dinner. It was Halloween night. At this restaurant, you could eat, you could dance, you could play backgammon. With Julio and me were Alfredo Fraile and Ramón Arcusa. It seemed to be a fine place, we were looking forward to going in, but an American at the door told us we couldn't enter because we weren't members. He had no idea who Julio Iglesias was. But all of a sudden, the doorman, a Cuban, recognized Julio and told the other gentleman about him. Then—in we went. It was a wonderful evening.

As a human being, he's a great person and I love him dearly. I have seen details on his part that have surprised me because he is such a busy man. Last year when he was here for his tour in Spain, he made certain that I had tickets and was invited to a dinner that was given afterwards.

Q: What do you think of the production of "To All the Girls I've Loved Before"?

EG: To tell the truth, he had to go back to Ramón Arcusa. Many people intervene and one has to know Julio. Julio is a perfectionist. And to put up with him, it's got to be Ramón Arcusa. Ramón understands him and has the right feeling. They get together and one says let's change this, and they'll change it fourteen times until they feel it's right. And, they always have great results.

Q: Who released his first record in the United States?

EG: It was Morris Levy of Roulette Records. Ivan Mogul was also involved in the negotiations. Mr. Levy believed in him. Later, his records were released by Alhambra records and now all the material has been re-released by CBS.

Q: To what do you attribute his success?

EG: Julio knows what he wants. That he may not always know how to express it musically is a different matter, but what he has is that incredible feeling. I have always said that Julio has been touched by God. That he sings better than anyone else, no. He is a combination of things. He doesn't bother anyone—not the mother, not the grandmother, not the child, not the husband. He is well received by the whole world. For his manner, he is embraced by the whole world. Julio is a great person.

A man couldn't feel that Julio is his enemy, even though he is very big. He awakens a maternal instinct in women. The majority of the women, despite wanting him as a man, would also like to have his head on their shoulders. He awakens the illusion for a woman to feel herself a mother, even though later she may prefer to be his lover. An older woman sees him as she would like to see her son: well educated and elegant.

Q: What do you think of his repertoire of recent years?

EG: His greatest hits have always been his own work. I don't know if he has the time or the peace of mind, the tranquility, to compose now as much as before. One of my favorites is "Abrázame," written by Rafael Ferro and Julio. To me, it's a "standard."

Q: How do you, personally, think of Julio Iglesias?

EG: He's a great person. I don't owe him and he doesn't owe me—we owe each other.

# THE

# DYNAMIC DUO,

MANUEL DE LA CALVA
AND RAMON ARCUSA

*M*anuel de la Calva and Ramón Arcusa performed together as the popular "Dúo Dinámico" (Dynamic Duo). Both have known Julio Iglesias since the very beginning of his career, and both have produced some of his records. Today, Maneul de la Calva and Ramón Arcusa are independent producers. They also head the Madrid music publishing firm of ACM Ediciones Musicales, together with Fernando Mitjavila. They gave this joint interview in Madrid in 1984.

Q: After Benidorm, when did your paths next cross with Julio Iglesias?

MC: It was in 1969. We bumped into him at yet another song festival, the one in Viña del Mar, Chile. We were invited guests at the festival, as the Dúo Dinámico. We were the ones who introduced Julio at the festival. Today he is perhaps one of the artists who sells the most in Chile, and is most loved by the Chileans.

Q: Did you like his voice, his style of singing?

MC: Yes. You know what happens, it bothers me to say things

after they've happened. But it's true. I can tell you, as a professional, I liked him from the very first. I have already commented on this with Ramón. And I'll tell you something else. "La Vida Sigue Igual" had many things going for it. The song itself. And Julio. And Los Gritos, the group that sang it with him at Benidorm. These young kids did it really well. Together with Julio, they made the song something special and it won.

I used to tell Ramón, "Look, he has something special in his voice that reminds me of Charles Aznavour." I think it must have been the way his voice trembles a bit. I'd tell Ramón that Julio really had something. The fact is, he had a lot.

Above all else, he has an iron will. He has a goal in life to get where he has gotten. To get it has cost him dearly. But he has succeeded. He is a phenomenon of self-discipline. He has changed through the years. If you look at photos from then, they have nothing to do with his photos now.

He is a very intelligent guy. He has said, "I'm going to West Germany . . . to America. . . ." Whatever he says, he does it. He has opened up markets and when he has opened them, he has been number one all over Europe and in other places too. He is intelligent, genuinely intelligent, and one has to acknowledge this.

Q: Which was the first of your songs that he recorded?

RA: "Soy Un Truhán, Soy Un Señor" (I Am a Rogue, I Am a Gentleman).

Q: And it sold well?

RA: Yes. It coincided with his changing of record companies. It was when he signed the contract with CBS Records. To Spain, it was Discos Columbia, but for the rest of the world it was CBS.

Q: When did you start producing Julio's records?

RA: Just a little after Manolo [Manuel de la Calva]. He had been producing his records for a few years at Discos Columbia, since he was then their Artistic Director.

I was working as an independent then, so we did this song and I started working with him. I wasn't sure if I wanted to work with him because my intuition told me that he was a very obsessive person. And, once you are in his circle, it would be difficult to get out. I had a feeling that once someone got in, there would be very little freedom. I started doing some arrangements and other songs. Before I realized it, I found myself involved in his productions. That first album was produced by Manolo and Julio and myself. A year later, after all the negotiations with CBS were completed, we were recording in Miami.

Q: Do you have any stories about Julio?

MC: About a year and a half ago, we were performing in a discotheque called Mr. Dollars in the outskirts of Madrid. A really beautiful place. Before we went on, Ramón looked at me and said, "I don't know why, but I have a feeling Julio is going to show." A while into the program, we see him peeking out from behind the sound equipment. So we told the audience that we were helping out this novice artist. He's a kid who is starting out and he may even remind you a little of Julio but any resemblance is purely coincidental.

Then he came out on stage and sang three songs with us. One was "Soy Un Truhán, Soy Un Señor." It was totally improvised, yet we all sang well together. We were given a standing ovation.

This sort of thing is very typical of him. He is very giving. Once he called me out of the blue and said, "Drop by my office in Madrid and pick up some airplane tickets you have waiting for you to Viña del Mar. Someone will meet you at the airport and take you to the hotel. Everything is paid for, so enjoy yourself." He doesn't have to do it, but he does it. It's been years since I've done something directly with him. I cooperate with Ramón by writing some songs, but that's it.

Sometimes I'm talking on the phone long distance with Ramón, and Julio will grab the phone away from him and ask how I'm doing and if I need anything. He's extraordinary.

Q: What's he like in the recording studio?

RA: He's a born worker. He is a perfectionist. He looks for perfection beyond anyone's understanding. There is always a better interpretation of a phrase, and he searches for it. No matter what he has done, he wants more. Everyone can say it's fantastic, but still he'll want to repeat and repeat and repeat until he finds the interpretation, precision, and sentiment he wants to give each word. I'll tell you, sometimes it escapes us. What may seem perfect to us, he'll want to repeat and repeat, and improve it. He has a very good sense of what he wants. That is the basic. He knows better than anyone what he wants, which is the same thing. At the end, it is through elimination that he finds what he wants. What he doesn't like, he eliminates. And the end, he finds what he likes. And what he likes has proven to be what the public likes around the world. Because he is very successful.

Q: What is his secret?

MC: For many people, success comes because they're intelligent, and they know what they want. Julio Iglesias is so intelligent that he would select the song of his worst enemy if he felt it would be a hit. I remember something he once told us. He said, "Don't think that I sing your songs because of friendship. Because of friendship, I will do whatever you want, but the songs, they are sacred. I sing your songs for my own personal interest. If not, I wouldn't sing them."

RA: I think it's knowing that what he likes coincides with what the public likes. He knows how to touch certain emotions when he sings. He knows how to reach everyone. That perfection he seeks, he knows how to reach certain feelings of the people just by a certain inflection in the voice, the emotion he puts in the voice.

Q: Has he changed much?

RA: I think he has changed a bit. It depends on the moment. I say this because I understand it has happened, but it has happened to us without our realizing it. It's according to situations. Where you are sometimes decides things, or your basic formulas will change in order to achieve certain things that were not at your reach before. There are times when he may appear more extroverted than others. It may happen to you. It happens to all of us.

In moments of tension he is crossing, especially at this moment in his career, this is natural. In his career, there has always been a challenge of another country, then another. And sometimes this continuous tension provokes him perhaps into a mental state that leaves something to be desired. But it's not hard to understand why this happens. It doesn't happen often.

Then, like anyone, he can have moments of euphoria.

In general, he really hasn't changed.

Q: What are his likes and dislikes?

RA: He likes simple things. He's happy with a hamburger.

I'll tell you a story about that. He had a masseuse who would prepare for him all sorts of juices and shakes. Healthy, healthy concoctions. In Los Angeles, it is very much in vogue to drink these things made of carrots, apples, pears, and I don't know what. This masseuse would prepare these drinks for him, and also special foods for his diet. Every day, she would prepare something and leave it in a little refrigerator that he would keep in his room. I guess that everything she whipped up ended up in the trash. But she never knew. When she would ask how it was, he would say, "Great. You know that drink with the apples? You can prepare it again for tonight."

Q: Who has helped Julio in his career?

MC: Julio has always surrounded himself with a very good team. They all work well together.

Q: Tell me a little about the album *1100 Bel Air Place*.

RA: Julio and I had worked together for close to seven years on six albums. Julio decided to make his leap to America. He thought that the best thing for a market that different, a different public than those he was used to, would be to have a producer who understood the American market. CBS, through Dick Asher, contacted Richard Perry. I was with them at their first meeting to assist in any way that I could. We wanted the meeting to go well. I liked Julio, and was interested to see that things went off without a hitch.

To me, it didn't matter if I became deeply involved or not. What did matter is that they had to find a producer who wasn't Latin. At least, that was what we first thought. We always said that Julio wouldn't change his style too much when he attempted the American market, that he shouldn't stop being Julio. Of course, he was running the risk with someone whose whole mission was to "think America," someone like Richard Perry, that he would do something that was totally alien to his own personality, that he wouldn't be able to find his style. If he changed his style drastically, he wouldn't be Julio Iglesias but someone else.

Richard Perry was the man who was going to do the job. After a year, they recorded around twelve to fourteen songs, but most of them were different from Julio's style. Julio then called and asked me to continue to work with him.

Q: The two of you have a song with Julio on the album. How about the Spanish album?

RA: This year, we don't have any songs. We didn't have the song or the luck or the inspiration to write a song for him this year.

Q: Did you think the first time that you saw him perform in Benidorm that he would do as well as he has?

RA: That he would go this far? No. To be honest, to have reached what he has reached—who could expect such a thing? It never occurred to me. I'm amazed. But on various occasions, he has said he was going to do something, some practically impossible thing, and before you know it, he has done it.

When we started selling in France, when he recorded his first French album, he said, "Give me a piece of paper." Then he went on to predict that he was going to sell 40,000 in the Netherlands, a million and a half in France, 400,000 in West Germany, and so on. And that the next year, he would sell five million records in Europe. At that moment, it was impossible to foresee what would happen. For a Spaniard to sell a million records in France is like selling the moon. But he did it.

Initially I really never thought that he would be so big, but by the second year with him, I believed everything. In other words, I understood. I understood that he had a strong internal desire and could achieve anything.

Q: Do you enjoy being a part of his team? Or would you prefer to do other things?

RA: I like it. I would be lying if I said that I didn't enjoy being a part of the team of someone who is so successful.

Q: What was it like when you used to record with Julio at Discos Columbia?

MC: Julio would show up the last three days after we had recorded the playbacks. We would all end up sleeping in the studio, spread out all over the chairs and couches until 9:00 A.M. the next day. After working on an album for the last nine months, he would come and whatever we had wasn't what he wanted. The only thing that was valid was the thing we did in the last month [with Julio present].

Q: Does this mean there's a method to his madness?

MC: The thing was that sometimes he had already placed the voices on nine of the songs and then on the tenth one he would notice something he felt wasn't right, that there was a different sound. Then he'd say, "Did you hear that?" And we'd do it over again. Sometimes he would find something wrong on one channel, which none of us could detect. So he would insist that we try it on another channel. We would try to fool him and record on the same channel. He always knew. We could never fool him.

RA: What he does in the last month is what stays. When it came to the American album, it was more than valid because obviously his pronunciation was better towards the end. For *1100 Bel Air Place*, he must have recorded some forty, forty-five songs. In general, we usually share the same opinions, but when it came to this album, there were many differences.

Q: What's next? After the U.S.A.?

MC: The spaceship *Challenger*? [Laughter.] With Julio's track record, one never knows.

# DISCOGRAPHY

*T*he following discography represents the Julio Iglesias albums released in English, Spanish, French, Italian, German, and Portuguese.

## ENGLISH

### *1100 Bel Air Place* (1984)

*Side 1*
"All of You" (Duet with Diana Ross)
–J. Iglesias–T. Renis–C. Weil–
"Two Lovers"
–P. Jabara–J. Asher–
"Bambou Medley"
"Il Tape sur des Bambous"
–M. Heron–P. Lavil–D. Barbelivien–
"Jamaica"
–J. Iglesias–M. Colombier–A. Hammond–
"The Air that I Breathe"
–A. Hammond–M. Hazelwood–
"The Last Time"
–J. Iglesias–M. De La Calva–R. Arcusa–M. Panzer–

*Side 2*
"Moonlight Lady"
–A. Hammond–C. B. Sager–
"When I Fall in Love"
–E. Heyman–V. Young–
"Me Va, Me Va"
–R. Ceratto–Eng. Lyrics: A. Hammond–
"If (E Poi)"
–D. Gates–
"To All the Girls I've Loved Before"
(Duet with Willie Nelson)
–A. Hammond–H. David–

## *Julio* (1983)

*Side 1*

"Non Si Vive Cosi (Italian)
(Can't Live Like This)
–Billion–Revaux–Belfiore–
"Amor" (Spanish/English)
–G. Ruiz–R. Lopez Mendez–
Eng. S. Skylar–
"Abraçame" (Portuguese)
(Wrap Your Arms Around Me)
–J. Iglesias–R. Ferro–R. Altalbouti–
"Ou Est Passée Ma Boheme?"
(Carefree Days)
–G. Roig–
"Begin the Beguine" (Spanish/English)
–C. Porter–Spanish Lyrics: J. Iglesias–

*Side 2*

"Hey" (English)
–J. Iglesias–G. Belfiore–M. Balducci–
R. Arcusa–Eng. Lyrics: N. Newell–
"Nostalgie" (French)
(Nostalgia)
–J. Iglesias–R. Arcusa–C. Lemesle–
"La Paloma" (Spanish)
(The Dove)
–J. Iglesias–R. Arcusa–
"Wo Bist Du" (German)
(Where are you)
–J. Iglesias–M. de la Calva–R.
Arcusa–M. Kunze–Trim–
"De Niña a Mujer" (Spanish)
(From Childhood to Womanhood)
–J. Iglesias–C. Enterria–T. Renis–R.
Arcusa–

# SPANISH

## *En Concierto* (two-record album) (1982)

*Side 1*

"Obertura"
"Begin the Beguine"
Volver a Empezar
–C. Porter–J. Iglesias–
"Pensami" (Jurame)
–M. Grever–G. Belfiore–
"Vivir a Dos"
–J. Iglesias–M. de la Calva–
R. Arcusa–
"Grande, Grande, Grande"
–A. Testa–T. Renis–J. Iglesias–
"Cantando a Francia"
    "Que Reste-t-il"
    –C. Trenet–L. Chauliac–Salabert–
    "La Vie en Rose"
    –L. Guy–E. Piaf–
    "La Mer"
    –C. Trenet–A. Lasry–
"Momentos"
–J. Iglesias–Tony Renis–R. Arcusa–

*Side 2*

"As Time Goes By" (De la película
*Casablanca*)
–Herman Hupfeld–
"Cantando a Latinoamerica" (I)
    "Sabor a Mi"–A. Carrillo–
    "Noche de Ronda"–M. T. Lara–
    "Cucurrucu Paloma"–T. Méndez–
"Homenaje a Cole Porter"
    "Night and Day"
    "True Love"
    "I Love Paris"
"Feelings"
–M. Albert–
"Hey"
–J. Iglesias–G. Belfiore–M. Balducci–
R. Arcusa–
"Nathalie"
–J. Iglesias–R. Arcusa–

*Side 3*
"Obertura"
"Quijote"
–J. Iglesias–M. de la Calva–
R. Arcusa–
"Fidele" (Amantes)
–J. Iglesias–M. Balducci–G. Belfiore–
R. Arcusa–J. Mercury–
"De Niña a Mujer"
–J. Iglesias–T. Renis–R. Arcusa–
"Ou Est Passée ma Boheme?"
"Quiereme Mucho" (Cantando por la
niña Vanessa)
–G. Roig–P. Carrell–
"Cantando a Latinoamerica" (II)
  "La Flor de la Canela"
  –C. Granda–
  "Moliendo Cafe"
  –J. Manzo–
  "Noches de Ypacarai"
  –Z. de Mirkin–
  "Guantanamera"
  –J. Fernandez–H. Angulo–
  P. Seeger–J. Marti–
"Quizas, Quizas, Quizas"
  –O. Farres–

*Side 4*
"Samba da Minha Terra"
–Dorival Caymmy–
"Un Canto a Galicia"
–J. Iglesias–
"Quando Tu N'es Plus La"
(Caminito)
–G. C. Coria Penaloza–J. de
Filiberto–P. Carrel–M. Jourdan–
"Un Sentimental"
–J. Iglesias–R. Ferro–R. Arcusa–
"Cantando a Mexico"
  "Ella"–J. A. Jimenez–
  "El Rey"–J. A. Jimenez–
  "Maria Bonita"–A. Lara–
"Me Olvide de Vivir"
–P. Billon–J. Revaux–J. Iglesias–R.
Arcusa–
"Paloma Blanca"
–Neneco Norton–

## *Momentos* (1981)

*Side 1*
"Nathalie"
–Julio Iglesias–Ramón Arcusa–
"Momentos"
–Julio Iglesias–Tony Renis–Ramón
Arcusa–
"La Paloma"
–Julio Iglesias–Ramón Arcusa–
"Las Cosas Que Tiene la Vida"
–Danny Daniel–
"Amor"
–Ricardo López–Gabriel Ruiz–

*Side 2*
"Quijote"
–Julio Iglesias–Manuel de la Calva–
Ramón Arcusa–Gianni Belfiore–
"No Me Vuelvo a Enamorar"
–Julio Iglesias–Fernán Martínez–
Ramón Arcusa–
"Con La Misma Piedra"
–Massias (Ketepao)–
"Esa Mujer"
–Julio Iglesias–Rafael Ferro–Fernán
Martínez–Ramón Arcusa–
"Si El Amor Llama a Tu Puerta"
–Ray Girado–

## De Niña A Mujer (1982)

**Side 1**
De Niña a Mujer"
–J. Iglesias–T. Renis–R. Arcusa–
"Volver a Empezar" (Begin the
beguine)
–Cole Porter–Vers. Esp. J. Iglesias–
"Después De Ti"
–J. Iglesias–M. de la Calva–
R. Arcusa–
"Que Nadie Sepa Mi Sufrir"
–E. Diezo–A. Cabral–
"Isla En El Sol" (Island in the Sun)
–H. Belafonte–Lord Burgess–J.
Iglesias

**Side 2**
"O Me Quieres O Me Dejas"
(Devaneos)–Luis Gardey–
"Y Pensar . . ."
–D. Ramos–J. Iglesias–
"Si, Madame"
–J. Iglesias–G. Belfiore–R. Arcusa–D.
Fariña–E. Picciotta–
"Grande, Grande, Grande"
–A. Testa–T. Renis–J. Iglesias–
"Como Tú"
–P. Trim–J. Iglesias–M. de la Calva–
R. Arcusa–

## Hey (1980)

**Side 1**
"Por Ella"
–J. Iglesias–M. de la Calva–R.
Arcusa–
"Amantes"
–J. Iglesias–M. Balducci–G. Belfiore–
R. Arcusa–
"Morriñas"
–J. Iglesias–R. Ferro–R. Arcusa–
"Viejas Tradiciones"
–A. Genovese–G. Belfiore–J. Iglesias
"Ron y Coca Cola"
–Amsterdam–Baron–Sullavan–J.
Iglesias–

**Side 2**
"Hey"
–J. Iglesias–G. Belfiore–M. Balducci–
R. Arcusa–
"Un Sentimental"
–J. Iglesias–R. Ferro–R. Arcusa–
"Paloma Blanca"
–Neneco Norton–
"La Nave del Olvido"
–Dino Ramos–
"Pajaro Chogüi"
–Pitagua–

## Emociones (1979)

*Side 1*
"Me Olvide de Vivir"
–Billon–Revaux–Adapt. Esp. J.
Iglesias–M. Korman–M. de la Calva–
R. Arcusa–J. Flores–
"Voy a Perder La Cabeza Por Tu
Amor"
–M. Alejandro–A. Magdalena–
"Spanish Girl"
–J. Iglesias–M. de la Calva–R.
Arcusa–
"Pobre Diablo"
–J. Iglesias–M. de la Calva–R.
Arcusa–
"Quiereme" (Basada en las Danzas
Polovtsianas de *EL PRINCIPE IGOR*)
–Borodin–Adapt.: J. Iglesias–M. de la
Calva–R. Arcusa–

*Side 2*
"Preguntale"
–J. Iglesias–M. de la Calva–R.
Arcusa–
"Quiereme Mucho"
–G. Roig–
"Con una Pinta Asi"
–J. Iglesias–J. L. Navarro–M. de la
Calva–R. Arcusa–
"No Vengo Ni Voy"
–D. Ramos–J. Iglesias–
"Un Dia Tu, Un Dia Yo"
–P. Trim–M. de la Calva–R. Arcusa–
J. Iglesias–

## Mi Vida en Canciones (two-record album) (1978)

*Side 1*
"Quiereme Mucho"
–G. Roig–
"Quiero"
–J. Iglesias–R. Ferro–Cecilia–
"Cuidado Amor"
–Livi–
"Abrazame"
–J. Iglesias–R. Ferro–
"Me Olvide de Vivir"
–Billion–Revaux–Adapt. Esp. J.
Iglesias–M. Korman–M. de la Calva–
R. Arcusa–J. Flores–
"Por un Poco de tu Amor"
–Gomez–Hammond–

*Side 2*
"A Veces Tu, a Veces Yo"
–J. Iglesias–Cecelia–
"Por El Amor de Una Mujer"
–D. Daniel–Sonny Marti–
"El Amor"
–Ferriére–Guichard–Carli–Iglesias–
"Sono Io"
–Anelli–Gargiulo–Adapt. Esp.
Iglesias–
"Un Canto a Galicia"
–J. Iglesias–
"A Flor de Piel"
–J. Iglesias–R. Ferro–

*Side 3*
"Soy un Truhan, Soy un Señor"
–M. de la Calva–R. Arcusa–J.
Iglesias–
"Candilejas" (Limelight)
–Chaplin–Parsons–
"Cu–cu–rru–cu–cu Paloma"
–T. Méndez–
"Quiereme" (Basada en las Danzas
Polovtsianas de *EL PRINCIPE IGOR*)
–Borodin–Adapt. J. Iglesias–M. de la
Calva–R. Arcusa–
"Alma Llanera"
–P. Elias Gutiérrez–
"Preguntale"
–J. Iglesias–M. de la Calva–R.
Arcusa–

*Side 4*
"Manuela"
–M. Alejandro–A. Magdalena–
"Pobre Diablo"
–J. Iglesias–M. de la Calva–R.
Arcusa–
"Jurame"
–M. Grever–
"Un Dia Tu un Dia Yo"
–P. Trim–M. de la Calva–R. Arcusa–
J. Iglesias–
"Caminito"
–G. Coria Penaloza–J. de D.
Filiberto–
"33 Años"
–J. Iglesias–

## A Mis 33 Anos (1977)

*Side 1*
"Soy un Truhan, Soy un Señor"
–De la Calva–Arcusa–Iglesias–
"Sono Io"
–Anelli–Gargiulo–Adapt. Esp.
Iglesias–
"Si Me Dejas No Vale"
(Si Mi Lasci Non Vale)
–Rossi–Belfiore–Adapt. Esp. J.
Iglesias–
"Por un Poco de Tu Amor"
–O. Gómez–A. Hammond–
"Un Gorrion Sentimental"
(Domani E Un Giorno in Piu)
–Balducci–Belfiore–Adapt. Esp. J.
Iglesias–

*Side 2*
"Seguire Mi Camino"
–Ramos–Iglesias–
"33 Años"
–Iglesias–
"Cada Dia Mas"
–De la Calva–Arcusa–Iglesias–
"¿Donde Estaras?"
–De la Calva–Arcusa–
"Good-Bye Amore Mio"
(Good-Bye A Modo Mio)
–Balducci–Belfiore–Adapt. Esp. J.
Iglesias–

## En El Olympia (1976)

**Side 1**
"Introduccion/Vivencias"
–Iglesias–Navarro–Prida–
"Un Canto a Galicia"
–J. Iglesias–
"Corazon, Corazon"
–J. A. Jiménez–
"Maria Bonita"
–Agustín Lara–

**Side 2**
"Manuela"
–M. Alejandro–A. Magdalena–
"Feelings"
–M. Albert–
"La Mer" ("El Mar")
–Trenet–Lasry–
"Minueto"
–J. Iglesias–R. Ruiz–

## America (1976)

**Side 1**
"Caminito"
–G. Coria Peñaloza–J. de D.
Filiberto–
"Recuerdos de Ypacarai"
–Z. de Mirkin–D. Ortiz–
"Historia de un Amor"
–C. Almaran–
"Obsesion"
–P. Flores–
"Sombras"
–C. Brito–R. Sansores–
"Mañana de Carnaval"
–A. Maria–L. Bonfa–

**Side**
"Jurame"
–M. Gerver–
"Guantanamera"
–J. Fernandez–H. Angulo–P. Seeger–
J. Marti–
"Vaya Con Dios"
–L. Russell–I. James–B. Pepper–
Adapt. A. Alpin–
"Moliendo Cafe"
–J. Manzo–
"Ay, Ay, Ay"
–O. Perez Freire–
"Alma Llanera"
–P. Elias Gutiérrez–

## A Mexico (1975)

**Side 1**
"Cu cu rru cu cu Paloma"
–Tomás Méndez–
"No Me Amenaces"
–José Alfredo Jimenez–
"Ella"
–José Alfredo Jimenez–
"Cuando Vivas Conmigo"
–José Alfredo Jimenez–
"Noche De Ronda"
–Maria Teresa Lara–

**Side 2**
"Solamente una Vez"
–Agustin Lara–
"Amaneci en Tus Brazos"
–José Alfredo Jiménez–
"Corazón, Corazón"
–José Alfredo Jimenez–
"De un Mundo Rara"
–José Alfredo Jimenez–
"María Bonita"
–Agustin Lara–

## El Amor (1975)

**Side 1**
"Abrazame"
–J. Iglesias–R. Ferro–
"A Veces Tu, A Veces Yo"
–J. Iglesias–Cecilia–
"Tema de Amor" (Love's Theme)
–Schroeder–White–
"Quien"
–J. Iglesias–R. Ferro–
"Cuidado Amor"
–Livi–

**Side**
"Quiero"
–J. Iglesias–R. Ferro–Cecilia–
"El Amor" (La Tendresse)
–Ferriere–Guichar–Carli–Iglesias–
"My Sweet Lord"
–G. Harrison–
"Dejala"
–J. Iglesias–R. Ferro–
"Candilejas"
–Chaplin–Parsons–

## A Flor de Piel (1974)

**Side 1**
"A Flor de Piel"
–J. Iglesias–R. Ferro–
"Vivir"
–D. Daniel–D. Hightower–Adapt
Esp. J. Iglesias–Cecilia–
"Dicen"
–J. Iglesias–Luis Franch–Cecilia–
"Manuela"
–M. Alejandro A. Magdalena–
"Un Adios a Media Voz"
–R. Ferro–J. Iglesias–Cecilia–

**Side 2**
"Te Quiero Asi"
–Don McLean–Adapt. Esp. J. M.
Pater–
"Por el Amor de una Mujer"
–Sonny Marti–Danny Daniel–
"Desde Que Tu Te Has Ido"
–Cecilia–
"Aun Me Queda la Esperanza"
–R. Ferro–J. E. Mochl–
"En Cualquier Parte"
–Mike Leander–Eddie Seago–Adapt.
Esp. J. Iglesias–

## Asi Nacemos (1973)

**Side 1**
"Asi Nacemos"
–M. Alejandro–A. Magdalena–
"Tenia una Guitarra"
–J. Iglesias–
"Bla, Bla, Bla"
–J. Iglesias–
"Hace unos Años"
–J. Iglesias–
"Alguien Que Paso"
–J. Iglesias–J. Pardo

**Side 2**
"Niña"
–M. Alejandro–A. Magdalena–
"A Chicago"
–J. Iglesias–
"Da Hil Sayo"
–J. Iglesias–
"No Es Verdad"
–J. Iglesias–
"24 Horas"
–J. Iglesias–J. L. Navarro–

## Rio Rebelde (1972)

*Side 1*
"A Veces Llegan Cartas"
–M. Alejandro–A. Magdalena–
"Hombre Solitario"
–R. Whittaker–
"A Veces Pregunto al Viento"
–J. Iglesias–
"Si Volvieras Otra Vez"
–J. Iglesias–Luis Franch–
"Yo Canto"
–J. Iglesias–

*Side 2*
"Rio Rebelde"
–Ch. Aguirre–R. Uballes–
"Sweet Caroline"
–N. Diamond–
"Cuando Vuelva a Amanecer
–J. Iglesias
"No Soy de Aqui"
–F. Cabral–
"Por una Mujer"
–J. Iglesias–

## Como el Alamo al Camino (1971)

*Side 1*
"Como el Alamo al Camino"
–J. Iglesias–
"Cuando Vuelva a Amanecer"
–J. Iglesias–
"En un Barrio Que Hay En La
Ciudad"
–J. Iglesias–
"Chiquilla"
–J. Iglesias–
"Gwendolyne"
–J. Iglesias–

*Side 2*
"Un Canto a Galicia"
–J. Iglesias–
"En un Rincon del Desvan"
–J. Iglesias–R. Farrán–
"Yo Canto"
–J. Iglesias–
"No Llores Mi Amor"
–J. Iglesias–
"La Vida Sigue Igual"
–J. Iglesias–

## Gwendolyne (1970)

*Side 1*
"Gwendolyne"
–J. Iglesias–
"Colinas Verdes"
–J. Iglesias–R. Ruiz Martin–
"Voy Siguiendo Mi Camino"
–J. Iglesias–
"Pequeñas Manzanas Verdes"
–Russell–
"Sentado a Beira Do Caminho"
–R. Carlos–E. Carlos–
"A Veces Pregunto al Viento"
–J. Iglesias–

*Side 2*
"Cuando Vuelva a Amanecer"
–J. Iglesias–
"Raindrops Keep Falling on My
Head"
–B. Bacharach–H. David–
"En un Burrito Orejon"
–C. Castillo–V. Schlichter–
"Ese Dia Llegara"
–M. Alejandro–
"Cantandole al Mar"
–J. Iglesias–

## *Soy* (1970)

*Side 1*
"Vivencias"
–J. Iglesias–J. L. Navarro–C. Prida–
"En Una Ciudad Cualquiera"
–J. Iglesias–
"Soy"
–J. Iglesias–
"Minueto"
–J. Iglesias–R. Ruiz–
"Mi Amor es Mas Joven Que Yo"
–Claudio Fontana–J. Iglesias–

*Side 2*
"Dieciseis Años"
–Danny Daniel–Sonny Marti
"Niña"
–M. Alejandro–A. Magdalena–
"Una Leyenda"
–J. Iglesias–
"Asi Nacemos"
–M. Alejandro–A. Magdalena–
"Vete Ya"
–J. Iglesias–J. L. Navarro–

## *Todos Los Dias un Día* (1969)

*Side 1*
"Todos Los Dias un Dia"
"Preguntale"
–J. Iglesias–M. de la Calva–R.
Arcusa–
"Moto-Persecucion"
"Perfidia"
–A. Dominguez–
"El Amor"
–Ferriere–Gulchard–Carly–
"Central Park"
"Un Dia Tu, Un Dia Yo"
–P. Trim–M. de la Calva–R. Arcusa–
J. Iglesias–
"En Chichicastenango"

*Side 2*
"Sola en la Ciudad"
"Abrazame"
–J. Iglesias–R. Ferro–Cecilia–
"Biscayne Bay"
"As Time Goes By"
–Herman Hupfeld–
"Isla Contadora"
"Me Olvide de Vivir"
 Billon Revaux–J. Iglesias–M.
Korman–M. de la Calva–R. Arcusa–J.
Flores–

### *Yo Canto* (1968)

*Side 1*
"La Vida Sigue Igual"
–J. Iglesias–
"Tenia Una Guitarra"
–J. Iglesias–
"Bla, Bla, Bla"
–J. Iglesias–
"El Viejo Pablo"
–J. Iglesias–
"Hace Unos Años"
–J. Iglesias–
"No Llores Mi Amor"
–J. Iglesias–

*Side 2*
"Gwendolyne"
–J. Iglesias–
"Alguien Que Paso"
–J. Iglesias–J. Pardo–
"Mis Recuerdos"
–J. Iglesias–
"Yo Canto"
–J. Iglesias–
"Lagrimas Tiene el Camino"
–J. Iglesias–
"Chiquilla"
–J. Iglesias–

# FRENCH

### *L'Amour Crea La Femme*

*Side 1*
"Don Quichotte" (Quijote)
–J. Iglesias–M. de la Calva–R.
Arcusa–G. Belfiore–M. Jourdan–P.
Carrel–
"Les Sourires de Mes Souvenirs"
(Momentos)
–J. Iglesias–T. Renis–R. Arcusa–C.
Lemesle–
"Amor, Amour, My Love" (Amor)
–R. Lopez–G. Ruiz–P. Carrel–
"D'Abord . . . Et Puis . . ."
(Recuerdo de Ipacarai)
–Z. de Mirkin–D. Oritz–P. Carrel–
"C'Est Bon Tout Ca" (Rum and Coca
Cola)
–M. Amsterdam–J. Sullavan–P.
Baron–M. Jourdan–P. Carrel–

*Side 2*
"Et L'Amour Crea La Femme"
(Si el Amor Llama a tu Puerta)
–R. Girado–M. Jourdan–P. Carrel–
"Nostalgie" (Nathalie)
–J. Iglesias–R. Arcusa–C. Lemesle–
"L'Amour Fragile" (Querer y Perder)
–R. Girado–P. Carrel–
"Ne Me Parle Plus D'Amour" (No
Me Vuelvo A Enamorar)
–J. Iglesias–F. Martinez–R. Arcusa–C.
Lemesle–
"Oh, La La L'Amour" (Con La
Misma Piedra)
–Massias (Ketepao)–P. Carrel–

## Fidele

*Side 1*
"Viens M'Embrasser"
–J. Iglesias–R. Ferro–M. Jourdan–
"Une Chanson Qui Revient"
–Cole Porter–M. Jourdan–
"Les Derobades"
–L. Gardey–Lemesle–
"L'amour au Grand Soleil"
–H. Belafonte–Lord Burgess–P.
Carrel–
"C'Est Toi Ma Chanson"
–J. Iglesias–T. Renis–R. Arcusa–C.
Lemesle–

*Side 2*
"Mon Pauvre Coeur"
–J. Iglesias–M. de la Calva–R.
Arcusa–M. Jourdan–
"L'Amour Est Fou, Madame"
–G. Belfiore–R. Arcusa–D. Farina–E.
Picciotta–P. Carrel–
"Tu Danses, Danses, Danses"
–A. Testa–T. Renis–C. Lemesle–
"Un Jour Tu Ris, Un Jour Tu
Pleures"
–F. Cabral–C. Lemesle–
"Fidele"
–J. Iglesias–M. Balducci–G. Belfiore–
R. Arcusa–J. Mercury–

## Sentimental

*Side 1*
"C'Est Ma Vie" (Jurame)
–M. Grever–P. Carrel–M. Jourdan–
"Elle" (Morriñas)
–R. Ferro–J. Iglesias–R. Arcusa–J.
Mercury–
"Je Chante" (Por Ella)
–M. de la Calva–J. Iglesias–R.
Arcusa–J. Mercury–
"Une Nuit de Carnaval" (Paloma
Blanca)
–N. Norton–J. Mercury–M. Jourdan–
"Ma Chance Et Ma Chanson" (La
Nave del Olvido)
–D. Ramos–M. Saisse–

*Side 2*
"Quand Tu N'es Plus La" (Caminito)
–Filiberto–P. Carrel–M. Jourdan–
"Sentimental" (Un Sentimental)
–J. Iglesias–R. Ferro–R. Arcusa–C.
Lemesle
"Il Faut Toujours un Perdant" (Hey)
–G. Belfiore–M. Balducci–J. Iglesias–
R. Arcusa–M. Jourdan–
"Jolie" (Pájaro Chogui)
–Pitagua–J. Mercury–M. Jourdan–
"J'ai Besoin d'un Peu D'Amour" (Por
un Poco De Tu Amor)
–Gómez–Hammond–J. Mercury–

## A Vous Les Femmes

*Side 1*
"Pauvres Diables" (Pobre Diablo)
–J. Iglesias–M. de la Calva–R.
Arcusa–M. Jourdan–
"L'Amour C'Est Quoi?" (Preguntale)
–J. Iglesias–M. de la Calva–R.
Arcusa–C. Lemesle–
"Les Traditions" (La nostra buona
educazione)
–G. Belfiore–A. Genovese–C.
Lemesle–
"Je N'Ai Pas Change" (No Vengo Ni
Voy)
–D. Ramos–J. Iglesias–C. Lemesle–
"Moi Je T'Aime" (Summer Love)
–Ph. Trim–M. de la Calva–R.
Arcusa–R. Bernet–

*Side 2*
"Ou Est Passée Ma Bohême?"
(Quiereme Mucho)
–G. Roig–M. Jourdan–
"Le Mal De Toi" (Voy a perder la
cabeza por tu amor)
–M. Alejandro–A. Magdalena–J.
Mercury–
"Souriez Madame" (Con una Pinta
Asi)
–J. Iglesias–J. L. Navarro–M. de la
Calva–R. Arcusa–M. Jourdan–
"Je L'Aime Encore" (Donde Estaras)
–M. de la Calva–R. Arcusa–M.
Jourdan–
"Un Jour C'est Toi, Un Jour C'est
Moi" (Give Me Your Love)
–Ph. Trim–M. de la Calva–R.
Arcusa–M. Jourdan–

## Aimer La Vie . . .

*Side 1*
"Aimer la Vie" (Soy un Truhan, Soy
un Señor)
–De la Calva–R. Arcusa–J. Iglesias–C.
Lemesle–
"Une Chanson Sentimentale" (Un
Gorrion Sentimental)
–G. Belfiore–Balducci–C. Lemesle–
"Ne T'en Va Pas Je T'aime" (Si Mi
Lasci Non Vale)
–G. Belfiore–Rossi–P. Delanoe–
"Amigo" (Gavilan o Paloma)
–R. Perez Botija–C. Lemesle–
"Tendre Voleur" (Good-bye a Modo
Mio)
–G. Belfiore–Balducci–C. Lemesle–

*Side 2*
"Le Monde Est Fou, Le Monde Est
Beau (A Veces Tu, A Veces Yo)
–A. Sobredo–J. Iglesias–C. Lemesle–
"A La Croisee des Chemins" (Seguire
mi Camino)
–D. Ramos–J. Iglesias–C. Lemesle–
"Mes Trente-Trois Ans" (33 Años)
–J. Iglesias–C. Lemesle–
"J'ai Besoin de Toi" (Cada Dia Mas)
–De la Calva–R. Arcusa–C. Lemesle–
"Stai" (Limelight)
–C. Chaplin–G. Belfiore–

# ITALIAN

## Amanti

*Side 1*
"Hey"
–G. Belfiore–J. Iglesias–M. Balducci–
R. Arcusa–
"Amanti"
–G. Belfiore–J. Iglesias–M. Balducci–
R. Arcusa–
"Insieme"
–G. Belfiore–J. Iglesias–M. de la
Calva–R. Arcusa–
"Dividila Con Me"
–G. Belfiore–R. Livi–
"Volo"
–G. Belfiore–J. Iglesias–R. Ferro–R.
Arcusa–

*Side 2*
"Chi E'Stato"
–G. Belfiore–D. Ramos–
"Un Sentimentale"
–G. Belfiore–J. Iglesias–R. Ferro–R.
Arcusa–
"Ritornare a Casa"
–G. Belfiore–J. de Filberto–F.
Peñaloza–
"Andiamo a Cena Fuori"
–G. Belfiore–J. Iglesias–D. Ramos–
"Cioui Cioui"
–G. Belfiore–Pitagua–

## Innamorarsi Alla Mia Eta

*Side 1*
"Non si Vive Cosi"
–Dillon–Renaux–Belfiore–
"Innamorarsi alla Mia Eta"
–Alejandro–Magdalena–Belfiore–
"Quasi un Santo"
–de la Calva–Arcusa–Iglesias–
Belfiore–
"La Nostra Buona Educazione"
–Genovese–Belfiore–
"Un Giorno Tu, Un Giorno Io"
–de la Calva–Trim–Arcusa–Belfiore–

*Side 2*
"Se Tornassi"
–Hammond–Gomez–Belfiore–
"A Meno Che"
–Iglesias–de la Calva–Arcusa–
Belfiore–
"Quando si Ama Davvero"
–Roig–Belfiore–
"Chi Mi Aspettava Non E'Piu'la' "
–Ramos–Belfiore–
"Amo Te"
–de la Calva–Trim–Arcusa–Belfiore–

121

## Momenti

**Side 1**
"Sono un Vagabondo"
–G. Belfiore–R. Arcusa–M. de la
Calva–J. Iglesias–
"La Donna Che Voglio"
–G. Belfiore–R. Ferro–F. Martinez–J.
Iglesias–
"Bella Bella"
–G. Belfiore–D. Ramos–
"Momenti"
–R. Arcusa–G. Belfiore–T. Renis–J.
Iglesias–
"Amor, Amor, Amor"
–G. Belfiore–G. Ruiz–R. Lopez–

**Side 2**
"Nathalie"
–G. Belfiore–R. Arcusa–J. Iglesias–
"Se L'Amore Se Ne Va"
–G. Belfiore–R. Arcusa–F. Martinez–
J. Iglesias–
"Venezia a Settembre"
–G. Belfiore–C. Porter–
"Avanti Tutta"
–G. Belfiore–F. Cabral–
"Arrangiati Amore"
–G. Belfiore–A. Cabral–E. Dizeo–

## Sono un Pirata, Sono un Signore

**Side 1**
"Pensami"
–Belfiore–M. Grever–
"Sono un Pirata, Sono un Signore"
–Belfiore–De la Calva–Arcusa–
Iglesias–
"Dove Sarai"
–Belfiore–De la Calva–Arcusa–
"Amico"
–Belfiore–Botija–
"Abbracciami"
–Belfiore–Iglesias–Ferro–

**Side 2**
"Restiamo Ancora Insieme"
–Belfiore–R. Girado–
"33 Anni"
–Belfiore–Iglesias–
"Seguiro' Il Mio Cammino"
–Belfiore–Ramos–Iglesias–
"Sono Sempre Io"
–Belfiore–De la Calva–Iglesias–
"Stai"
–Belfiore–Ardo–Chaplin–

## *Da Manuela a Pensami* (two-record album)

*Side 1*
"Manuela"
–D. Pace–M. Alejandro–A.
Magdalena–
"Da Quando Sei Tornata"
–M. Coppola–Cecilia–
"Bimba"
–R. Arnaldi–M. Alejandro–A.
Magdalena–
"Quella di Sempre"
–A. Salerno–M. Alejandro–A.
Magdalena–
"Caminito"
–G. Coria Penaloza–J. de D.
Filiberto–

*Side 2*
"Se Mi Lasci Non Vale"
–L. Rossi–G. Belfiore–
"A Eleonora Perche' E' Un Fiore"
–Belfiore–Livi–
"Anima Ribelle"
–G. Belfiore–J. Iglesias–R. Ferro–
"Non Rimane Che un Addio"
–M. Coppola–R. Ferro–J. Iglesias–
Cecilia–
"Solamente una Vez"
–Agustin Lara–

*Side 3*
"Sono un Pirata, Sono un Signore"
–G. Belfiore–De la Calva–Arcusa–
Iglesias–
"Un Amore a Matita"
–G. Belfiore–J. Iglesias–R. Ferro–
"Restiamo Ancora Insieme"
–Belfiore–R. Girado–
"Passar Di Mano"
–G. Belfiore–D. Daniel–S. Marti–
"Guantanamera"
–J. Fernandez–J. Angulo–P. Seeger–J.
Marti–

*Side 4*
"Pensami"
–G. Belfiore–M. Grever–
"Piccole Grandi Cose"
–G. Calabrese–J. Iglesias–R. Ferro–
"La Ragazza di Ypacarai"
–G. Belfiore–Z. De Mirkin–D. Ortiz–
"Quel Punto in Piu"
–G. Belfiore–J. Iglesias–Cecilia–
"De un Mundo Raro"
–José Alfredo Jimenez–

# GERMAN

## *Zartlichkeiten*

### Side 1

"Mit Tranen in Den Augen Ist Man Blind"
–J. Iglesias–Belfiore–Balducci–Arcusa–dt. text: Michael Kunze–
"Ich Hab' Gelacht, Ich Hab' Geweint" (Un Jour Tu Ris, un Jour Tu Pleures)
–Cabral–Lemesle–dt. text: Michael Kunze–
"Eine Rose, Die Nie Welkt (Por un Poco de Tu Amor)
–Gomez–Hammond–dt. text: Michael Kunze–

"Amigo, Ich Wollt'immer Ein Adler Sein" (Gavilan O Paloma)
–R. Pérez Botija–dt. text: Michael Kunze–
"Bleib Bei Mir Bis Zum Morgen (Para Que No Me Olvides)
–Cirado–dt. text: Michael Kunze–

### Side 2

"Wo Bist Du" (Como Tu)
–Trim–Iglesias–de la Calva–Arcusa–dt. text: Michael Kunze–
"Du Bist Mein Erster Gedanke" (Quiereme Mucho)
–Roig–dt. text: Ralph Maria Siegel–
". . . Aber Der Traum War Sehr Schon" (When They Begin the Beguine)
–Porter–Iglesias–dt. text: Michael Kunze–
"Island in the Sun" (Wo Meine Sonne Scheint)
–Belafonte–Burgess–dt. text: Kurt Feltz–

"Sie War Da" (Jurame)
–Grever–dt. text: Michael Kunze–

# PORTUGUESE

## Minhas Cancoes Preferidas

*Side 1*
"Hey" (Hey)
—J. Iglesias—G. Belfiore—M. Balducci—
R. Arcusa—Fernando Adour—
"Pobre Diablo" (Pobre Diablo)
—J. Iglesias—M. de la Calva—R.
Arcusa—Fred Jorge—
"Me Esqueci de Viver" (J'ai Oublie de Vivre)
—Billon—Revaux—J. Iglesias—Fernando Adour—
"Não Venho Nem Vou" (No Vengo Ni Voy)
—D. Ramos—Fernando Adour—
"Inesquecivel Boemia" (Quiereme Mucho)
—G. Roig—Fernando Adour—

*Side 2*
"A Menos Que" (Preguntale)
—J. Iglesias—M. de la Calva—R.
Arcusa—Fernando Adour—
"Camiñito" (Caminito)
—G. Peñaloza—J. de Filiberto—Fernando Adour—
"Velhas Tradiçoes" (La Nostra)
—A. Genovese—G. Belfiore—J. Iglesias—Fernando Adour—
"Por Ella" (Por Ella)
—J. Iglesias—M. de la Calva—R.
Arcusa—Fernando Adour—
"Por Você" (Summer Love)
—P. Trim—M. de la Calva—R. Arcusa—Fernando Adour—

## As Vezes Tu, As Vezes Eu

*Side 1*
"Ãs Vezes Tu, Ãs Vezes Eu"
—J. Iglesias—Cecilia—F. Adour—
"O Amor"
—Ferriere—Guichard—Carli—J. Iglesias—F. Adour—
"Seguirei Meu Caminho"
—Ramos—J. Iglesias—F. Adour—
"Amigo"
—R. Pérez Botija—Ernesto Escudero—
"Onde Estarâs?"
—de la Calva—Arcusa—F. Adour—

*Side 2*
"Sou Um Charlatão, Sou Um Senhor"
—de la Calva—Arcusa—J. Iglesias—F. Adour—
"Vem"
—Charles Chaplin—F. Adour—
"Se Me Deixas, Nao Vale"
—Rossi—Belfiore—Adapt. J. Iglesias—F. Adour—
"Quero"
—J. Iglesias—R. Ferro—Cecilia—F. Adour—
"Jura—Me"
—Maria Grever—F. Adour—

International Fan Club
Amigos De Julio
4500 Biscayne Boulevard
Suite 333
Miami, Florida 33137

*About the Author*

ELIZABETH GARCIA has had extensive experience, including publicity and promotional writing, in the international music world. She was in charge of artist relations in the First and Second Latin International Song Festivals in New York, and has collaborated in the domestic and international promotion of Brazilian recording artist Morris Albert (composer of "Feelings").

While active in the International Division of SOM Industria e Comercio S.A. in Brazil, Ms. García worked with Discos Columbia, Julio Iglesias' first label, and witnessed the strategy behind his ultimate conquests of different countries.

Presently she collaborates as a music reviewer for the Spanish periodical *El Tiempo*. Through her continued involvement in the music world, she maintains close contact with artists, managers, disc jockeys, producers, critics, promoters, publicists, photographers and others whose work was invaluable in compiling this book.